To Kim—
Enjoy the Journey

Suddenly Psychic: Core Messages to Enhance Your Psychic Journey

Gregory A. Kompes

FABULIST FLASH PUBLISHING, LTD.

Printed in the United States of America

ISBN 10
0-9793612-2-2

ISBN 13
978-0-9793612-2-7

Library of Congress Control Number: 2010924685

Fabulist Flash Publishing, Ltd
PO Box 570368
Las Vegas, Nevada, 89157
www.YourPsychicJourney.com

Dedicated to Todd Isbell...
...Love is an amazing gift.

Contents

Contents

Contents

Contents

Suddenly Psychic:

Core Messages to Enhance Your Psychic Journey

Introduction

In 2007, while I sat in a session at a writer's conference, the speaker, author and psychic Victoria Laurie, made a comment about deadlines: "It's not like you can tell your editor that your Uncle Jack died and you need an extension." Everyone in the room laughed; I felt a chill run down my spine.

After the session, I found Victoria in the hall and approached her. We said hello to each other, and I began. "It's really strange. I did have an Uncle Jack who died, and I used that to gain a much needed extension on my book deadline." Victoria smiled at me. "Further more, I didn't go to the funeral, but used that time to finish my book."

"He was your uncle. I wondered where that comment came from," she said. Victoria went on to do a brief psychic reading and answered my nagging question about how my uncle felt about me using him like that and not attending his funeral. He found it funny, by the way, and was glad to be of service.

Victoria had said she wouldn't be giving any psychic readings during her weekend at the writer's event. She was there as an author and faculty member, not as a psychic. I felt honored to have received my mini reading with my uncle and was happy to provide any favor that I could to Victoria.

At the conclusion of the conference events a few days later, many of us who attended agreed to meet at a bar in the hotel. As I approached our small group, Victoria had "save me" eyes. I asked her and another woman if I could join them. Victoria seemed pleased, the other woman unhappy. Turns out, the woman was trying to finagle a reading out of Victoria. My joining them ended that conversation.

Without comment, Victoria shifted seats at our table and sat directly across from me. She said: "Your family is incredibly loud. They're not giving me any choice but to share the messages they have for you." She proceeded to do an extensive reading that centered around my paternal grandparents, primarily my grandfather. At the end of her reading Victoria said, "Now I know why I had to come to this conference. I rarely attend conferences, but something urged me to be here for this one."

When the reading was over, I looked around, and the woman I'd "saved" Victoria from was nowhere to be seen. For a second time that weekend, I had been honored by receiving a reading from Victoria Laurie.

I'd always wanted to meet my grandfather. But, I was born in February 1966, and he died in December of that same year. I was the only grandchild in that family with no memory of the man. I'd spent a lot of my life wondering about him and asking about him. No one offered much information. The bits and pieces I picked up over my life didn't really fit together well. In the process of trying to know him, I'd become a musician, as he had been; although, I turned the hobby into a career for about ten years.

After Victoria's reading for me, I called several of my aunts. I shared what I had learned from the psychic author, and my aunts in turn told me many more stories about my grandfather. I'd always thought of him as James, but it turns out he went by Jimmy. As other stories came out, I discovered that I had taken on many of his traits over my own lifetime, down to the clothes I liked to wear and the foods and beverages I preferred.

Among the many things Victoria shared with me that Saturday night was the fact that my grandfather spent a lot of time looking over my shoulder. He found my writing funny a lot of the time. And, he was incredibly proud of me. At this moment, like the moment when Victoria shared the sentiment, a wonderful rush of love and emotion rushes over me. The difference today is that I know that rush of feeling is an energetic hug from my beloved and long-departed grandfather, Jimmy.

As I continue to research the psychic world and expand my own psychic skills, abilities, and connections,

I'm discovering that late onset psychic awareness is becoming more common.

Another wonderful experience for me is the discovery that many of the people I share psychic readings with begin to expand their own psychic and spiritual journeys after we spend time together, much like the experience I had after I received a psychic reading from the gifted Victoria Laurie. Although, not everyone I come across totally changes their life path in the discovery. That's what I have done. I canceled the previous career directions and paths I'd been pursuing and went headstrong toward my psychic gifts. But, those I'm meeting now who have discovered their own psychic connections late in life are using their abilities to advance their lives and careers in positive ways.

It is because of my experiences and studies that I have been prompted to write this book. Along my own psychic journey, I've met my team of guides. Everyone, whether they're aware of it or not, have a team of guides and angels helping and assisting them throughout their lives. And, interestingly, we often welcome new guides and angels and say good-bye to others as we travel our life journey. We'll talk more about them later in these pages.

If you've read other books on psychic gifts and abilities, you'll notice that many of the authors give designation to when their psychic entities are chiming in. We won't be doing that here. While generously laced with words, ideas, and concepts from The Three Sisters and other members of my team, the voice of this text is mine.

The main goal of this book is to assist those who find themselves suddenly psychic. You are not alone in the sudden discovery of your abilities. There are many just like you and many more to follow. My intention in these pages is to help anyone interested in moving forward on their psychic journey.

Throughout this book, I introduce and explore a series of Core Messages to help you enhance psychic skills and abilities. The Core Messages will also help you better understand how our world operates and how we fit into and help expand our universe. The Core Messages were introduced to me by my collection of guides, angels, and the spirit entities that I've come into contact with through my own experiences of meditation and the public, private, and personal psychic readings that I've experienced with friends, family, and clients.

I find the term "psychic reading" to be a bit weird. But, it is the accepted phrase that psychics have used for generations. The reason it may not be the best phrase to describe sharing information gained through our psychic connection is because not everyone sees words or symbols during their psychic connection. Some of us hear our guides and some are also intuitives, those who just know information. We'll talk in more detail about the different types of psychic experiences. So, while the word "reading" may not best fit all of us, it is the accepted word, the common word, so I'll use it throughout this book.

Along our journey together, I'll be sharing snippets

of my own experience of becoming suddenly psychic. The sudden discovery of my psychic abilities and the development of my skills happened rapidly for me. The most interesting discovery though has been that, while I feel like these are new skills and abilities, there have been traces of them throughout my life. It turns out that all of this isn't new to me; instead, it's been an experience of discovery and fine tuning the skills that I already had. And, I suspect, if you've found yourself to be suddenly psychic, that this is probably going to be true for you, too.

As we continue deeper into this great time of psychic and spiritual awakening there will be large numbers who find themselves suddenly psychic. And, you, having been among us early on during this time, will be slightly ahead of the trend. This will allow you to become a model to those who discover their abilities after you. Through experience and resources, everyone has the power to become Suddenly Psychic!

The Core Messages

The way I like to explain messages and symbols is that they're like shorthand. They sum up larger ideas and concepts in a few words. This makes them easy to understand and remember. Along my psychic journey, I've received a collection of core messages from my team of spirit guides and angels that form the foundation of my psychic awareness. Throughout the core messages, I include antidotes, stories, and experiences that I've had on my own and with some of the folks I've performed psychic readings for. I share these core messages so you can better understand your personal psychic connection and spiritual journey.

Core Message #1
Everyone is Psychic

The place to begin our psychic journey of psychic understanding together is first to accept that everyone is psychic. Everyone. You may not have previously used that word to describe yourself. Most haven't. After all, many think of psychics as those crazy ladies in layers of oversized jewelry and scarves who set up tables or tents at fairs and carnivals. Psychics are those folks with tables in New Orleans' Jackson Square or in dusty store fronts with neon signs, right?

I'm not going to tell you that everyone who says they're a psychic actually has the skills to help others using their psychic ability. That just wouldn't be true. But, I say with confidence that everyone does have psychic abilities, and everyone has the ability to explore and expand those abilities and skills. Our manner of dress and personality quirks have nothing to do with our psychic connection.

What is a Psychic Connection?

A psychic connection is the ability to connect and communicate with our personal spirit guides and angels. Such communication creates a bond and information stream between us and a group of spiritual entities who are not in physical form. We'll go into much greater detail in the messages that follow to explain who these entities are and why they're available to us. For this early moment, just know that a connection exists between us and them. This connection was chosen and established while we were still in pure source energy. Furthermore, the connection works whether we acknowledge it or not. That's the agreement we made before we began our current physical life.

When we're aware of and tapped into our psychic connection, we have access to information that will help our lives run smoother. When we connect with our team through our psychic abilities we also have immediate help when needed. When we connect through our psychic abilities, we are tapping into source energy, the place we all come from before our physical lives begin, and the place we return to when our physical lives end. This is the energy that is the source of all life and everything else that surrounds us.

Another great advantage of expanding and growing our psychic connection is that we not only tap into greater awareness and information about our lives, we also tap into an infinite source of pure, positive, nonjudgmental love. Our spirit guides, inner self, and angels all love us unconditionally. They never judge us. They never place expectations on us. Instead, they are all there to support and love us throughout our lives without question or exception. For many of us, the connection and bond we have with our team may be the only time we get to experience true, unconditional love. Having access to those feelings is probably the best reason to become strongly connected to our non-physical, energy-based, spiritual team.

Easy examples to explain how we're psychic are our gut reactions, first impressions, and intuition. How often have we said, "I don't know why, but I like her," or "It just doesn't feel right." We don't have a logical "reason" for these thoughts or feelings, but deep down, in our gut, we just know they're true. We just know. Somehow, we know more about the situation than the current information or logic tells us.

We all have these intuitive abilities. There's something that tells us that an impression is true. It might be explained because of that little voice in our head or a feeling in our bodies. Whatever the source, we know that the something is true.

We hear it and say it often: "Trust your gut." Or, in hindsight, "You should have gone with your first impression."

Those feelings, those knowings, those moments of intuition are us connecting in a psychic way to information provided by our spirit guides.

Our knee-jerk, gut reactions and feelings are not

just instinctual experiences. Instead, they are a way for our spirit guides to make contact with us, especially if we haven't developed our psychic connections in a deeper way. It's the job of our spirit guides to help direct us toward what is best for us. We've made an agreement with them to do so.

Of course, some of our quick, situational reactions are also learned. We've been taught to look both ways before crossing the street and have learned through teaching and experience not to touch a hot stove. Because of our learning, our reactions in such situations seem instinctual. They're not. They have been taught to us or learned by us through example and experience.

What's important is to understand that we've all got a personal connection to our spirit guides, angels, and our inner self who provide information when that information will best help us on the journey through this physical life. It's also important to know that with a little effort we can effectively learn to tap into that information when we want to. We don't have to wait for an extreme situation. It's also good to know that whether we attempt to build a strong connection with our team of guides or not they will continue to help us move forward through our physical life in the most positive way they possibly can.

Core Message #2
It's Normal to be Psychic

Since everyone is psychic, the next step forward on our psychic journey is to accept that it's normal to have these abilities. Based on societal labeling, if the majority agree or have a trait, they become the dominant group. Since we've all got psychic abilities and connections, it stands to absolute reason that it's normal to be psychic.

Where I think we get off track based on labels is the connection of psychic skill and the term paranormal. Paranormal is the wrong word for what goes on. After all, if everyone has this ability, it's more normal than not to have psychic experiences. From this point forward, we'll treat the subject of our psychic abilities and connections as just that, normal.

When I first discovered my psychic abilities during a trip to Ohio, I was excited. Yet, afterward, I became cautious. I didn't want to tell anyone beyond my partner, Todd. I phoned him from the bar where those first psychic intuitive moments happened. During those early readings, I lost track of all time. When we took a break from the reading, I picked up the cell phone and called him, forgetting the three hour time difference between where I was and Las Vegas. He dutifully answered the phone, checked to see that I was okay, and listened to me ramble on about the experience I'd just had. Of course, when we talked the next day, he barely remembered our conversation because it occurred at 4:00 in the morning!

Beyond Todd, I didn't tell anyone. I had to explore this. I wanted to find out more. Maybe, this experience was just a fluke. And, when I finally did decide to tell my friends and family, I did it in small, baby steps. It was like coming out of the closet all over again.

Lucky for me, my friends and family are used to me taking off in new directions and following obscure life path decisions. I'd dropped out of college the first time around to be a full-time musician. I moved to new places on whims. I changed jobs, returned to school, took up writing and poetry, and have explored many other jobs and paths. My friends and family learned early to always write my address and phone number in pencil. So, when I did announce that I was psychic, well, they just erased the previous job title and wrote the new one in.

Whether you choose to tell others about your psychic connection is your choice. Whatever you decide, remember that you're not alone in having a psychic connection.

Core Message #3
Psychic Journeys are Spiritual Journeys

I spent a good portion of my life feeling rebellion toward organized religion. My childhood religious experiences in a Catholic home were mostly negative. I did enjoy the ceremony, the candles and incense, and the music. What bothered me were the messages taught about judging others and that some belonged and were allowed and others weren't. It bothered me that I wasn't allowed to feel any differently about my spirituality than what the priests or my parents taught me. That concept just didn't feel right to me.

Because I'm gay, the church would only welcome me if I conformed to what they said was right. When I left my parents' home, I also left the Catholic Church. I knew that I had a deep spiritual connection. I believed in something greater than myself at work in the universe, creating the universe. Yet, the Catholic teachings didn't support the way I felt about spirituality. I've never believed that we could easily place the concepts of spirituality inside a tight set of rules.

Spirituality, in my young opinion, needed and required freedom. It was an individual choice between us and whatever that energy was where we came from.

Those feelings, and the personal freedom I received when I turned 18, launched me onto a personal spiritual journey. At first, because it was a model I understood, I tried to find a religious group that would welcome me and also allow me to find my own way. I tried all the organized religions. I read extensively about eastern cults, philosophies, and cultures. Along the way I found myself picking and plucking the concepts and beliefs from each group that made sense to me and worked for my own growing and changing belief system.

Where I ended up was a discovery that it wasn't the teachings of many religions that bothered me, but the interpretations. The desire held by organizations that we conform to their version of the teachings of the historic spiritual philosophers while making financial contributions week after week to keep those teachings going. It bothered me that each group felt there was only one way, their way, to believe in the great universe we call home.

I abandoned all of the organized groups. I didn't abandon my spirituality, but instead departed from other's interpretation of spirituality. By casting off the old, I allowed room for the new.

I ended up with a spiritual foundation that a universal energy was the source of all life. I guess I'd stripped my spiritual beliefs to the bare bottom. I was comfortable with that. When I discovered the Law of

Attraction, not the watered down version on Oprah or in The Secret, but the full-blown, based on vibration version of Law of Attraction taught by Abraham (via Esther and Jerry Hicks), I felt that I'd found what I was looking for. I'd found something that made sense to the core of my spiritual being. Something that explained the universe, built off my simple spiritual foundation, and allowed me the power and control of my spiritual journey without any judgments.

As my psychic connection grows, I sometimes talk to my team about the big questions of the universe. They've reinforced that the Law of Attraction is the only law of the universe of importance to those of us in physical. They've supported and explained that we are all spiritual beings, some of us spending time in physical at this moment. Those of us in physical, while in a different form than pure source energy, remain source energy ourselves, and we will return to that place of source energy when our time in physical is completed. And, that we in physical have total and absolute control of the experience that we have during our current lifetime.

Now, this doesn't mean that you need to strip away all of your own spiritual beliefs to be psychic or build a psychic connection. Quite the contrary. We are each on a life journey that is both a physical experience and a spiritual one. The beauty of our experience is that we are not only allowed, but encouraged to go in the directions that we choose, no matter what that direction turns out to be.

What we do need to accept is that our psychic journey, like our life journey, is a spiritual journey. There are great forces in the universe that are at work around us. How we choose to interact with them, that's totally up to us. There is no rule book beyond the one that we write for ourselves.

Of course, being a spiritual journey that we are in control of, it is possible that some of your current belief systems and ideas may be challenged as you continue forward. For me, that's always been a good thing. For others, this may be more difficult.

Understanding and believing that the psychic journey is also a spiritual journey really isn't necessary to move forward on your own psychic journey. It's one of those puzzle pieces that's good to have in the mix. Just because it's in the box doesn't mean we have to take it out and place it anywhere in the picture we're creating of our physical lives.

Core Message #4
Physical Death Isn't the End of Our Spiritual Journey

One of the main reasons that it's normal to be psychic is because physical death isn't the end of our journey. Our life does not begin when we take on our physical shell, nor does it end when we cast off our physical shell. We are vibrational energy that chooses to spend a bit of time in the physical, Earthbound experience.

I just don't believe in death. When you spend your day talking to spirits, angels, guides, and those who were here in physical form, but aren't anymore, but who may also be planning their return or reincarnation, it's impossible to believe that there's some sort of end just because we "die." Sure, we leave our physical bodies behind at the end of this physical experience, but time in physical is simply another step on our spiritual and energy-based journey. Because of this, I find being a bit disrespectful of death is a good thing.

So many of us give the concept of death way too much importance and power. Why? Because we've been taught to do so, usually when we're children. It's time to let go of some of our early learning when it comes to life and death.

To be fair, it makes sense that our parents and early caregivers taught us to avoid death. It's their role after all. It's the agreement our parents made when they decided to have children: keep them safe and get them through to adulthood. Of course, some of our caregivers were better at this than others, but the basics are there: look both ways before crossing the street; don't touch the hot stove; wear your seatbelt; eat this/don't eat that.

Much of that early learning still works well for us today, like looking before we cross the street. Even with the words, most of us touched the stove to see what the big deal was about. We jumped off the garage roof to see if we might be the one who could fly. We avoided foods they said were good for us and did our best to consume more sweets than we had permission to eat. Many of us roll through those stop signs when there isn't any other traffic (or a cop) around.

Why do we break the rules? Words don't teach, experience teaches. We must try things for ourselves. We have to have the experience to know what does and doesn't work for us.

We come into our current lives for the joy of the experience, plain and simple. We know when we arrive that our time here is limited. We also know that when our time here is over we'll reemerge fully into our spiritual- and energy-based reality. In the interim, between arriving and leaving, there is one basic truth: Life is supposed to be fun. We're supposed to enjoy this experience with as much exuberance as possible. Those early caregivers, along with those we give up our power to today (teachers, bosses, family members, ministers, etc.), have different ideas. They want us to conform. They want us to live the lives they say are "correct" or "proper."

To them I offer a smirk. This life is our life. We chose to be here, We made that choice because we wanted to explore and expand our possibilities. We're here because we wanted to come into the physical, learn and grow, and have fun with the experience.

It's time to lighten up, to laugh more, and worry less. Physical death isn't something to be feared. It's just our end of time in physical. Our energy never ends. In fact, because of our time here among the living, it expands and grows stronger.

It's time to revive the old mantra: If it feels good, do it.

The concept that physical death is not an end is one of the most challenging for many who have suddenly psychic experiences. Everyone must shift their thinking to allow for the concept that the self we are existed before we became physical beings, and that same self continues on after what we humans call death. The cause for this challenge is primarily organized religion. While most of the world's religions offer some explanation of life after death, they've created images and symbols that are askew from reality.

Think back to your high school chemistry class and the concept that energy can't be created or destroyed, it only changes form. That's exactly what we're talking about here. Our personal energy, including our individual personality, does not stop when our physical life ceases. When our physical journey has been completed, we release the shell (our physical body) we've been using during our physical lifetime. At that moment, we transition fully and reemerge with our pure energy and spiritual source.

Because we are continuous in our experiences, there are some personal connections that we maintain and strengthen over time. One of these connections is to our true energy, often called our inner self. When we are born into our physical bodies our personal energy gives us the things we think of as ourselves. These include our thoughts, emotions, and ultimately our personalities. These personal traits stay with us over time and experience as we make the loop back and forth between pure energy experience and the physical experience when we are born into a body here on Earth.

A fascinating fact is that while we inhabit our physical bodies, a part of us (from an energy standpoint) remains back on the energy source side. This is our inner self. In fact, the greater part of who we are remains in that source energy place; it's rather like we're tethered between the physical and source energy worlds. Another way to explain how our energy is in two places at once is the image of a pie. Think of yourself like you are a complete pie. When in physical form on Earth it's as if we've removed a single sliver of that pie and brought it with us. After we transition out of physical form, back into pure energy, our pie will once again be whole.

When we end our physical journey, all of our energy regroups in a single energy form once again. That is, until we decide to return to another physical experience. It's true, we come back again and again, by choice, to have different life experiences over and over. Our life is an ongoing experience, sometimes like a loop that brings us back to physical and returns us again to pure energy again and again.

A final example to explain our life journey, from energy to physical and back again is the oft used rollercoaster image. We line up, find a seat, and begin the journey. It's slow at times, exciting at others. We're scared at times and thrilled at others. We scream, we laugh, our hearts pound and race. Some rollercoaster rides are exciting, others not. When we arrive at the end of the ride, and while the ride is over, we are still living. We transition from the ride experience back to our energy life. Because of the experience and their related emotions, we're a little changed. Now, we have the choice. We can queue up for another ride or not. We can visit a different amusement park or not. We have the choice and free will of what rides at what parks we choose. No matter what we choose, we are us, although a more experienced version.

So, instead of the word death, let's use the word transition. We never end our journey, we just transition from experience to experience.

Core Message #5
We All have
Absolute Free Will

There is no such thing as a predestined life. We have absolute free will during our entire journey. This includes both our times here in the physical world and our time in source energy.

The concept that we have free will is a difficult concept for many. Anyone raised with beliefs that stem out of any type of organized religion may find it challenging to believe that we choose our life, create our life, and live our life based on the choices and decisions that we make.

Having free will means that we not only make choices and decisions for ourselves, but that each choice or decision we make determines the direction we travel and the final outcome we experience.

While others may act or be required to fulfill our wants and desires, these others act in cooperation with our own wants and desires. They act and cooperate because of the influence of our spiritual guides and their own. We come together and interact with others because of what we want and what is mutually desired. We are free at any moment to change our wants and desires and to therefore change the direction of our life path.

Core Message #6
We are Personally Responsible for All Aspects of Our Life

Along with accepting that we have free will means that we also must accept that we have absolute responsibility for the life we create, the actions that we take, and the thoughts that we think. How we choose to live and express our lives is up to us, but we must accept too that, because we choose to create our life, we are also responsible for all aspects of our life. There are no victims in the physical or spiritual worlds.

This core philosophy is related and deeply connected to the Law of Attraction as taught by Abraham, a group of spiritual entities channeled by Esther Hicks. Interest in and understanding of the universal Law of Attraction has experienced a reemergence because of the work and effort of Esther and her husband Jerry Hicks (see the resource section for more information). At this moment, the information provided by Esther is the most current and comprehensive information available on the powerful Law of Attraction. I extend great love and thanks to Abraham, and the work of Esther and Jerry for sharing the teachings of Abraham.

Because the Law of Attraction is at the core of everything in our lives, it is also an incredibly positive foundation for building our psychic connection and is, therefore, worth exploring and understanding. The basic message of Law of Attraction is "like attracts like." We manifest or create our own lives based on our thoughts and emotions and the vibrations those thoughts and emotions create in the universe. We are what we think. Our emotions are the immediate indicators of whether our thoughts align with who we are and who we are becoming. If we feel good and excited about life, we're doing the correct things. When we don't feel well emotionally or physically, it's an indication that we have veered from the most positive path for us at that time in our physical life. The more passionate we are about our thoughts, and the better we feel, the greater the creation. Best of all, nothing we ever choose is wrong. Each decision and desire simply brings us more experience, growth, and learning.

Law of Attraction: An Example

My partner, Todd, loves extreme weather. Living in Las Vegas, we barely have any weather at all. It's either sunny and hot or sunny and cold here in the desert. So, for him to have weather experiences, he turns to shows on the Weather Channel. Among his favorites is Storm Chasers. While watching a few recent episodes with him, I couldn't help but see Law of Attraction in action.

In Storm Chasers, scientists, meteorologists, film makers, and general crazy people visit the Midwest during tornado season. They chase these weather phenomenons for the thrill, science, and images that tornados create. I couldn't help notice that the young, excited, passionate chasers are the ones who are almost always in exactly the right place at the right time to experience and film tornados. These boys are juxtaposed by an older film maker who usually has a negative attitude and is almost never in the right place to get the film footage he wants. And, if he does happen to be in the correct location, other factors, such as lighting or bad roads keep him from obtaining the film footage he desires. This is an excellent example of the universal Law of Attraction in action.

Because we are responsible for all aspects of our lives, we, therefore, must approach our psychic connection in a responsible way. Our team is there to guide and assist us in anyway we want. It is up to us to choose what to do with the knowledge and assistance provided by our team. As the saying goes: Be careful what you ask for, because you will surely get it.

We are always exactly where we're supposed to be.

Because of the powerful Law of Attraction, we create all the experiences we have in our life, whether we're aware of it or not. It is, therefore, because of the Law of Attraction that we are always exactly where we're supposed to be. Everything that happens in our lives happens because we created it. Where we have arrived at today is because of the thoughts, dreams, and expectations we have. With this knowledge, and because we have absolute free will that allows us to make any choice or think any thought, it's therefore possible to create exactly what we want for ourselves in the future.

Core Message #7
We Establish Our Boundaries

There are no moral or ethical rules that "must" be followed when participating in the spiritual and energy world. The vast majority of all rules and laws that have been created have little or even nothing to do with how the spiritual universe operates. The rules and laws that exist are instead related to the social environment we live our physical lives in. Most of these laws and rules benefit some while excluding others. They are boundaries that have been created by others, usually out of a fear or a desire for power.

In our own reality, we create our own boundaries. We decide what is right for us and what is the best path to follow to attain what we want. Our wants may be material or spiritual. Neither of these is better than the other. Instead, they are absolutely connected. We as individuals are energetically connected to all other beings, entities, and worlds. It is this connection that allows for our psychic connections between each other. Because everything is energy, everything is connected.

This connection of us to everything else is why boundaries are at times necessary. We decide how we want to live our lives and who we want to interact with during that living. Our spirit guides are here to help us with that living. And, they're also here to help us establish our boundaries within the energy world.

It is a fear of some that if they explore their psychic connections they'll allow negative or dark energies into their lives. Some even believe in demonic entities or spirits and that by opening up to their psychic connection, they will inadvertently become possessed by such a dark energy. Again, I stress that we establish our own boundaries. We decide what we want. And, we have absolute control over our life and the experience we have.

I have made agreements with my team of guides that whenever I connect with them it is only for the best possible outcome for me. I also have an agreement with them that when I do psychic readings of any kind that only those with positive messages may communicate with and through me. Because of this agreement, I do not encounter negative or dark energy. In fact, because of my agreement with my team, I never even consider that anyone with negative energy or goals not in line with my own will even approach me. We set our own boundaries, and we are responsible for those boundaries. Plus, we have a team of spirit guides ready and willing to help us set and maintain those positive boundaries and positive experiences.

Core Message #8 You're Not Alone on Your Psychic Journey

As mentioned earlier, some things we've been taught and have learned are helpful and benefit our well-being—like looking both ways before crossing a street. There are other things that we've been taught that aren't as beneficial. Many of the teachings we encounter as children and young adults deny our personal, spiritual connection; we're taught to deny the intuitive and psychic knowledge that all of us have access to. Instead of being taught to trust our own inner knowledge, we are asked to trust the words and ideas of others (parents, priests, ministers, teachers) without challenge or question. We're taught that, because our teachers and parents are older and more experienced, they know what is best for us. By trusting the knowledge of others and denying our own experience, we're doomed to following rules created by others instead of creating the rules that work best for us. Many rules and beliefs, because they haven't been updated over time, are now out of date.

It's not that we should live our lives alone, without the input or experience of others. Instead, it's that we want to learn to trust ourselves and the intuitive knowledge we have access to. This information comes from pure source energy, the source of all knowledge and experience.

We've established that we return to physical experience on Earth over and over when we choose to do so. Throughout these many lifetimes of experience, both in physical and in energy, we develop long- and short-term relationships with other energy entities. We make agreements with some of them before we return to a new physical experience. These agreements are primarily about having their support, love, aid, and assistance, because we know that in most of our physical journeys we won't remember that we're from the source of pure love and energy. We know from experience that we'll require help navigating the physical experience.

This is why each and every person currently living on the planet has at least one spirit guide. In fact, most of us have several or even a team of guides helping us along our journey. These entities reside in the energy world commonly referred to as "the other side" or "the great beyond." While not the best descriptions, they're what we've got.

We aren't assigned spirit guides, but rather select them ourselves before we are born into our physical lives. We've made an agreement, a pact if you will, that those we've chosen will aid and assist us from their unique, all-knowing vantage point.

Personally, I find our spirit guides to be the coolest part of our physical lives. Whether we develop our psychic connection to them or not, they're with us. While it's to our personal benefit to develop a strong connection to our team, it's not a requirement. And, best of all, it's their "job" to do all that they can for us in the most positive, loving way possible, whether we know they're there and acknowledge them, or not.

Love is a key point. Our guides, spirits, and angels all love us, unconditionally. They have no expectations of us, but instead simply love us and do all they can to help us achieve our own personal wants and desires, no matter what those wants and desires are. Pretty wonderful, huh?

Our spirit guides come in many different images and roles. Some are intelligent, loving beings, others are family and friends we've known in this lifetime who have transitioned back to source energy. Still others are angels and archangels.

Our guides also appear to us in different forms. Some will look, in our mind's eye, like people, others like beautiful lights; some will take the shape or form of animals, and others like great winged angels. There's no limit to their possible forms, shapes, colors, or styles.

I've compared notes with several of my psychic friends (can't help but think of those Dionne Warwick commercials whenever I say "psychic friends") and many of us have experienced guides who are very thin and incredibly tall. Another discovery is that two of my friends and I all share the assistance of the

Archangel Michael.

We'll explore spirit guides in more depth later in these messages. The important thing to understand at this point is that we all have spirit guides ready at any moment to aid and assist us. And, if our current desire is to grow and strengthen our psychic connection with them, they're thrilled to help us accomplish that, too.

My Team of Guides

In the beginning, as I discovered my team member by member, each offered a unique voice as well as a physical sensation to let me know who was speaking or providing guidance. As my skills advanced and my psychic hearing improved, they began speaking to me in a single voice. Now, I can listen to them as a single entity or seek them out as individuals. The choice is mine.

Jimmy

The first guide I met is my grandfather, Jimmy. He died ten months after I was born. I spent a lifetime lamenting that I didn't know him only to discover he's been standing over my shoulder, providing love, support, and guidance my entire life.

Victoria Laurie introduced him to me, and we discovered that he's always looking over my shoulder with love, support, and humor. I like knowing he's there. And, it was my introduction to Jimmy that helped me open my psychic connection and meet my other guides.

The Archangel Michael

I got very excited when I discovered that one of my active guides is the Archangel Michael. He appears to me as very, very tall. His positive loving energy always feels like a hug. He's also got large wings, which I've had the opportunity to have wrapped around me several times, which is the most loving feeling I've ever experienced.

What I've been finding so interesting is that several of my now close psychic friends also have Michael as their Archangel. It was curious to me at first that so many people in my life, those in tune with their psychic abilities and those not quite so in touch, share the same guide.

I talked to Michael about this several times. Those on the other side are excellent Multitaskers. So, for them, it's easy to be with many people at the same time; it's easy for them to assist, talk to, guide, and gently nudge multitudes of folks at the same time.

In this experience and many others that I've had, I'm gaining a deeper understanding that we are all energy and that energy really is absolutely connected. This connection not only allows our guides and those on the other side to be in many places at once, but millions of places at the same time. This same energy connection also allows us to be connected to everyone and everything in the universe and beyond at the same time. Pretty wonderful, really.

Brad

Brad was the third guide that I met. He's a high level teacher who continues to introduce new topics and experiences for me. We frequently meet in lovely nature settings like in the mountains with a wonderful verdant valley view or in comfortable chairs on the beach looking out over crystal blue waters.

The Three Sisters

Among my guides are entities who call themselves The Three Sisters. The Three Sisters were daughters and wives within the Sabine tribe and the Sabine families that ruled near what is now Rome. In fact, the second king of Rome was a Sabine. The sisters also originated the order known as the Vestal Virgins of Rome and reincarnated back into the role of Vestals over and over throughout that order's history. Much has been written about the Vestal Virgins throughout Western history, but the most important item is that the Vestals were the keepers of the Light of Rome. While this flame came to represent Rome's power and influence, the keepers of the light concept is much older. While the flame may be a representation, the light itself is the light of our Source.

While on vacation in Rome, before I'd discovered and developed my psychic gifts, I visited the Roman Forum and other antiquity sites on the Palatine Hill. I felt like I was at home, like I knew the place. It wasn't from pictures or postcards. Instead, I felt like I knew my way around. In my mind's eye I could see the original buildings—long ago decayed or destroyed. When I came to the original site of the House of the Vestals, I could see the colonnade. I could feel the energy of the priestesses who had walked on these stones before me. I felt a strong kinship. And, though there's little there now to see, I simply didn't want to leave.

Of course, I know now that I had come home in some way. The Three Sisters had directed my steps to those locations. They were trying to make a stronger contact with me than we'd yet had. Now that I've met them, now that The Three Sisters are a part of my daily life, I know them better. And, I have those feelings and memories, along with the visions they supplied, as symbols and keys to our life-long connection.

Peter

Of no religious or historic connection that I've yet discovered, Peter is my universe coordinator. All of our guides, and those they work with on our behalf, coordinate pieces of the universe for us. They nudge our impulses and direction so that we meet the people who will be most helpful to us. They help us navigate traffic. They get us in the right place at the right time, basically. Of course, we have to be receptive, and we have to listen to their suggestions to experience the full benefit of their actions.

While all our guides do take part in this, I've been connected with a guide who has the role in my life of coordinator. Peter is a new guide for me. He just revealed himself prior to my writing this book. I have to admit I don't yet fully comprehend his role in my life. But, I know he's there, and I know he's influencing in a positive way my desire to have the biggest life possible.

Core Message #9
The Psychic Foundation

There are four concepts that form the basic foundation of our psychic connection: Open Mind, Open Heart, Open Spirit, and Release of Fear.

Open Mind

In the early forming of our psychic connection, it helps tremendously to have an open mind. There will be many times along your journey where you'll wonder "is this real?" Usually, the answer is "Yes!" Until we establish and understand our connection, until we know our spiritual and psychic teams well enough to trust that they are real it helps to maintain the attitude of an open mind. There are times, both early in our psychic journeys and well into them, that our team of spirit guides may challenge us to help us grow a stronger bond and connection to them. Having an open mind and a little playfulness about our psychic connection will help us deepen that connection.

Open Heart

When we live our physical experience from a place of love, we improve our experience in countless ways. Most experiences in life go better when we approach them with an open, loving heart. The psychic connection is no exception. The connection we have with our spirit team is solely based on love. Our guides and all other spirit entities that we come in contact with come to us from a supportive and loving place. They connect with us to help us improve our life experience in a positive way. The information and messages they convey to us always, without exception, are delivered with love.

The best way to describe the place where our team resides is pure love. This is true not only for our psychic team, but for all the transitioned physical souls, as well.

No matter what happens with our psychic connection, no matter whom we communicate with on the other side, or even the trapped and lost souls we may encounter lingering on in our physical world are best approached from a place of love and positive energy.

Open Spirit

Our spirit, that inner self who motivates us and supports us, no matter what happens in the outside world, is the "real" us. Our spirit is the little voice inside of us who talks us through life. It's the part of us that keeps us safe throughout our life. Over time, as we experience life with all the joy and pain our journey brings, our inner spirit may become tighter and more protective. After all, who wants to be exposed to the negative emotions of life over and over?

Our inner self, being our protector, can sometimes become a bit skittish about the outside world and about new ideas and concepts. The familiar ways of being and thinking, while they may not be the best for us anymore, are comfortable, like that old pair of sneakers or that worn out sweatshirt that makes us feel good.

At first, it may be a little difficult to introduce the idea of your psychic connection into your every day thinking. To have the best experience with our psychic team, we must open our spirit to the experience. I've found the best way to do this is to come at our psychic connections from a playful attitude. Connecting with our team is a playful experience. As discussed above, our connection is centered on love. When we feel love, especially true, pure love, love without expectation, it's almost impossible not to enjoy the feeling. When we're feeling so loved and supported, it's also easy to smile and find the joy of the experience.

While it may be a challenge in the early stages of developing our psychic connection, it's worth it to open our spirit to the experience. When our spirit is open to our psychic connection, that connection will grow very strong. The strong connection will bring more love and joy into our life. That in turn will help grow our connection even stronger. And, so on.

Release of Fear

The unknown is generally the only cause of fear we ever face. Because we don't know what's going to happen next, we feel we don't have a personal experience reference point. Without that, our inner spirit, because it wants to keep us safe, offers up a fear reaction to the new or different situation.

This fear reaction does serve a positive purpose in our life. For example, it keeps us from walking too close to the edges of cliffs or from driving to fast on slippery, dark roads.

Sadly, our fear reaction can also keep us from having new and exciting experiences. So many times, our established fears come from negative experiences we had as children, before we had much of our own life experience to gauge whether what we're afraid of is actually something to be afraid of. What may have been a useful fear reaction as children, may not serve us well as adults, but because the fear is so ingrained into us, it can be difficult to release that fear. If we have a fear of heights, we may never see the amazing view from the top floor of a skyscraper. If we have a fear of water, we may never enjoy a boat ride. If we have a fear of flying, we may never visit exciting and exotic places around the globe.

Fear reactions don't only reside around physical experiences. Many fear reactions are also connected to our belief system. If we've been raised to believe that there is a devil or a place called Hell, we alter our actions and thoughts to accommodate that belief. Sadly, like those out-dated, physical fear reactions from our childhoods, many of the conceptual and belief fears are unfounded.

As adults who are in complete control of our lives and beliefs, it's good to question and explore different thought patterns that will help us face and release our fear reactions when they're no longer necessary or appropriate for the life we're living.

As we explore our psychic connection, it may be necessary to review and release old beliefs that are counter to the experiences we're having now. The interesting thing about beliefs is that they are only chronic patterns of thought. Like releasing the emotional hold of past experiences, we can release the emotional hold of past beliefs.

Beliefs, even those held by vast majorities of people, are often discovered to be incorrect. Two big examples from history: While most Europeans and Western thinkers believed the world was flat and you could fall off the edge, Columbus and other seafarers of the age proved that the world was round; While most in the world believed that all the planets and sun rotated around the Earth in perfect circles, Galileo proved that the planets actually rotate around the Sun in ellipse patterns.

It's good to explore and challenge our beliefs. It's the only way to discover if those beliefs work for us at this time in our physical journey. The best way to do this is to release our fears about challenging and changing our beliefs.

Where I've had the best success of releasing my

fears, especially fears connected to challenging my out-dated beliefs, is by acknowledging and accepting that I'm afraid of something. I accept it fully. Next, I set the belief aside in my mind, assuring myself that I can return to the belief I'm challenging if I decide that it's best for me. Finally, I assure myself that no one ever needs to know that I'm currently challenging a concept, belief, or fear.

Core Message #10
Our Psychic Connection Requires Intention

It is essential as you develop your psychic connection that you also decide on your intention, on why you're developing your personal psychic connection. Understanding your intention will help your team help you in building a stronger connection. It's also very important to note that your intention can change as your psychic connection changes.

A few early intentions might be as simple as:

"I want...

- ...to develop my psychic awareness."
- ...a positive psychic experience."
- ...to meet my spirit guide."
- ...to meet my guardian angel."

By setting your intention, by voicing the reason you want to have a psychic experience, your experience is more likely to be a positive one for you. Without setting an intention, your team of spirit guides doesn't have a clear goal to nudge you toward. Instead, they have to do the best they can to interpret where you are and what you want. They are always offering the best information and messages to help you, but if you're not open to hearing them, you won't. This often leads to them helping you achieve something and you not seeing clearly where you are, which can lead to frustration and a negative experience. A negative experience will not help you strengthen your connection.

Have you ever been looking at the night sky with a friend and the friend asks: "Did you see that shooting star?" Of course, if you didn't, by the time you look to the correct location, the shooting star is long gone. Our teams send us messages and information just like shooting stars, and we want to do our best to be looking in the right place to experience them.

As your psychic connection grows, your desire for what you want from your psychic experience will change or alter. It's absolutely acceptable to keep changing your intention. As long as you make clear what you want from your team, they will do everything they can to help you achieve the experience.

It's worth noting that it's best to be kind and gentle with ourselves on our psychic journey. When it doesn't seem to go the direction we want, it's easy to feel disappointment or frustration. These negative emotions are never helpful, not in life or along our psychic journey. It's best to have a little faith, that if we ask our team for something, they will do all they can to help us attain it. While cliché, it works: Rome wasn't built in a day.

Establishing, strengthening, and building a solid psychic connection takes time. Help your team help you by being easy about it. Be loving and supportive of them and of yourself.

Core Message #11
Our Spirit Guides and Angels are Multitaskers

In working with my team of spirit guides, I've come to understand that anything is possible in their realm. They exist without linear time. In fact, they exist without the construct of time or space at all.

With this base knowledge, I posed the question to my guides: "Can we be in two places at one time?" Their answer: "Yes." We all, without question or doubt, are excellent Multitaskers.

While doing a reading recently, we were talking to a client's father. He'd transitioned back to source many years ago. As we talked to him, I discovered that he'd already reincarnated. So, here we were talking to him, while at the same time, he's a "different" person here in the physical world. Here was another Multitasker at work.

This got me wondering about the aid we receive from our guides and spirits. Since so many are working for us in so many different ways at one time, how is it possible? In fact, as I've met psychics and intuitives here in the physical world, we've discovered that several of us share the same angel. How is this possible? The answer, our guides and spirits are excellent Multitaskers. They're quite capable (and enjoy!) being in more than one place at one time.

Core Message #12
There's No One Way to be Psychic

As I began to explore what psychics were, what they did, and how they performed, I quickly discovered that there's no one single way to be psychic. How we connect with the information and how we receive the information is as unique as we are.

I often find myself thinking that it would be so much easier to just have a textbook or informational DVD. We could all watch it, learn the skills, and be psychic. That's not the case. And, what I know now is that's a good thing. Getting to the information, meeting our team of guides, angels, and whatever other spirits or entities we have a connection to isn't all this journey is about. I think the discovery of how we connect with our team is a major part of our psychic and spiritual journey.

Because this all happened to me so suddenly, I did what most of us do, I headed to the internet and began searching for information. That's where all kinds of new words popped up for me: intuitive, clairaudient, clairvoyant, clairsentient, etc. It was a lot to take in at one time.

I read the content of dozens of websites. I can't begin to tell you which ones. If you've ever searched the internet, you know that those early searches are random. I kept changing the keywords of the searches as a new concept or idea that I didn't understand was introduced.

One of the most important realizations I had was that everyone who wrote about and experienced psychic connections did it in their own way. And, I just knew that it didn't matter at first what tools I decided to work with to explore this newfound ability. What did matter was that I was interested and excited about exploring it.

Another experience I had during all those internet searches was a knowing that I'd know what content and information was right for me when I came across it. I suspect that those reading this book feel that way about the messages and information contained within its covers.

Where I arrived knowing I had found the correct information for me was at Max Highstein's Website. (See Suddenly Psychic Resources for more information.) Max offers a course called Intuition Retreat that's a combination of written text and guided meditation. I ordered this course and can tell you that it worked very well for me in exploring and expanding my own psychic abilities.

As you continue on your psychic journey, trust those feelings you have. It's your intuition telling you "this is it" and "you've found it."

Core Message #13
Discover What Type of Psychic You Are

There are two main types of psychics: Mediums and Channels. Mediums are the more common. That's where the psychic is in the middle between the spiritual entity (guides, angels, or dead folk) and the physical world. The vast majority of psychics fall into this category. We hear, see, feel, or know the information being shared. We translate it and then share it with others. Even when it's just us and our team of guides, we are still considered a medium. In essence, we receive information from our team and "share" it with ourselves.

The vast majority of the psychics I know are mediums. They receive information and share it. That's how I work most of the time as well. I know, hear, see, or feel information and can share it with others. It's also the method I use to have direct conversations with my team of spirit guides and angels. I can see them and hear them. When I perform readings for others, there are often others added to the mix of those sharing the information I receive, like dead relatives and departed pets.

Channels work quite differently. When psychics channel, they move out of the way on a conscious level and let the entity or spirit energy use them as a communication tool. This isn't like being possessed, although some outsiders might call it that. Instead, the psychic is so tuned in to the energy realm, their vibration is so high, that they are able to release their resistance and move out of the way on a mental, conscious level.

There are very few channels working today whose names you would know. While she chooses to use other words to describe it, Esther Hicks is among the more famous channels. Esther chooses to say she's a "translator" when she receives information from Abraham, a group of energy level entities. I think the word channel is appropriate here. Esther moves out of the way on a conscious level and allows Abraham to speak and gesture through her. Another famous channel in recent history is Jane Roberts. Jane channeled an entity known as Seth. In the cases of both Abraham and Seth, the messages shared by these entities is on a grander level than most "average" psychics. Abraham and Seth both shared information and messages on a personal level, but also on a higher level of how we fit in the universe and how the universe operates. I like to think of them both as teachers.

Of course, one of the most famous channels of the twentieth century is Edgar Cayce. Cayce is often credited as the father of psychic awareness in the modern age. He was able to easily go into a trance state and answer any question that was asked of him. Cayce frequently used his ability to offer medical treatments and healings, even though he had no knowledge of medicine. He also made broad predictions about the future of the planet and our physical experience, as well as answered questions of a personal nature for people. Cayce's thousands of readings are housed at Edgar Cayce Association for Research and Enlightenment in Virginia Beach, Virginia.

An interesting thing about the channels I'm familiar with is that they don't remember the words spoken while they are channeling. Cayce always had his wife or secretary with him to take notes. Likewise, Jane Roberts' husband took dictation, although for Jane and for Esther Hicks, they have had the advantage of modern technology. Both Jane and Esther have collections of recordings of the work they have done while in the state of channeling their entities.

There's more information on Cayce, Hicks, and Roberts in the Resource section at the end of this book.

At the time of this writing, I am primarily a medium. I'm aware and conscious when receiving information. Although, I have had a few channel experiences with my team. I've very much enjoyed these experiences and do hope to have more of them in the future. What I find fun is that during the channel experience my voice and mannerisms change. I can feel that the experience I'm having is very different from the "usual" psychic medium experience I'm used to. It's also interesting to me that when in a state of channeling I'm still conscious, but find myself in a somewhat different mental or conscious place. It was as if my conscious mind separated a little from the rest of my body. I was able to lightly observe what I was doing, while at the same time, while verbally speaking to the group, I was also having a private conversation with my team.

There's no reason to fear any type of possession during either the psychic medium or psychic channel experience. We set our boundaries. We set our intentions. When these boundaries and intentions are created with positive love, our team keeps us in a place of only positive experience. This doesn't mean that some of the information we receive might not be difficult material for us or, in the case of readings for others, for the people we're performing a reading for. Sometimes, we need to share and deal with difficult topics and information, because those are the best messages, the most helpful messages to be shared at that time. Remember that we are in absolute control at all times of the positive experience we have when performing psychic readings of any type and in any fashion.

Core Message #14
Discover Which Psychic Methods Work Best for You

There are many methods of psychic communication. No one type works for everyone. A few of the most popular styles include Clairvoyant, Clairaudient, Clairsentient, and Intuitive. Although, most of us discover we utilize a combination of these skills. It's like being left-handed, but of course, having the ability to also use our right hands, too.

Clairvoyant

Clairvoyant psychics see images and symbols. Where do they see them? These pictures are seen in the mind's eye. Some psychics I know say they see the images as if a movie is playing on a screen in their mind. I've sampled different guided meditation examples that help build a screening room in our mind that acts as a place we can go in our mind to view these images.

While this is a very common psychic style, it's not

the only method. As I was building my own psychic connection, I expected to start seeing these mind movies. I felt disappointed for a time that I wasn't able to see them or develop the ability to see in the way others described.

As time has progressed, I do now occasionally see flashes of images or symbols, but I see them differently from how described by others. Instead of seeing them like a movie, I just know the scene or symbol that I'm seeing exists.

Clairaudient

Being clairaudient means you can hear the messages being shared by your team. This may manifest like hearing a voice in your head. It may also come through like a voice almost whispering in your ear.

Clairsentient

Clairsentient psychics can feel physical sensations. These may be slight and light, like feeling the emotions of someone else. The feelings may be stronger, like knowing how someone died because you can feel a pain in your chest or head.

While clairsentients are aware of the physical and emotional feelings that are part of the message, the pain is rarely actually experienced. You may know that someone coming through died of a heart attack, but that doesn't mean you'll experience a heart attack too while you share the message. Instead, you know what the pain felt like for the transitioned and you can share that.

I've found that emotions can be a bit different. Frequently for me, when the transitioned entity has a message of love or a heartfelt apology, I'll find myself welling up with emotion, often having tears come into my eyes during the reading. One of the realities during these times is that the emotional message I'm sharing, while important for the person I'm providing the reading for, also has a deep connection in my own emotional life. These experiences tend to be like watching those holiday Folgers coffee commercials that bring tears to the eyes of many of us.

Intuitive

For psychic intuitives, the message sharing doesn't come through symbol, sound, sight, or feeling. Instead, they just know the message or information. In the beginning, this can feel a little mentally rattling. There's a common question that comes up: "How do you know that?" And, the answer will be: "I just do."

Intuitive is at the core of my own psychic style. It's as if the information is simply transferred or uploaded to me, and I share the messages as I know them.

The Combo Psychic

It's common for psychics to not have a single message influence of just one of these types. Instead, we often receive messages through all the different styles.

That said, it's also common for psychics to have a dominant personal style, a core style that's the most comfortable. This personal style is then enhanced by the other styles.

Using my own experience as an example, I started out with a dominant intuitive style. I just seemed to know things. Looking back over my physical lifetime, I know that I've experienced and used information received in an intuitive way for a long time, long before I "discovered" my psychic ability. But, when I did open and strengthen my connection to my team of guides, I also began receiving some pictures and symbols that I could see. I started hearing them clearly and have been able to have direct conversations with my team. I frequently feel messages, too, especially emotional messages of love and apology.

Another thing I've learned is that it's become fun to play with my team to develop my message receiving skills. Once I got over my disappointment at not seeing pictures and images the way other psychics said they received them, I started developing my own style of clairvoyant psychic connection.

Core Message #15
Take Your Psychic Journey at Your Own Pace

Just as there's no one way to be psychic, there's also no correct rate of speed to develop your psychic abilities. There's no reason to rush the process of opening up your psychic doors, connections, and channels. In fact, rushing the development process can be detrimental to your psychic growth.

The most important realization is that we all travel our life journey at our own pace. What's right for one might not work for another. Seeing comparisons between skills can be helpful, because it can help us see where we'd like to go or what the possibilities of our abilities may lead to. But, that's where the positive use of the comparison of self to others ends.

Like so many things in our life we must have the experience ourselves before we learn from it. Swimming is an excellent metaphor here. We can read all the books we want, but its not until we dip our toes in the water and try it out that we truly learn how to do it. Building our psychic connection is exactly the same. We want to establish our connection and then build it stronger. It's an experience between us and our guides, and each relationship is unique.

Core Message #16
No Special Tools are Required

Many of us have images of those scarf-wearing women gazing into crystal balls to predict the future. We've all seen tarot card readers turning over fancy cards that they interpreted with messages from beyond.

My own guides have repeatedly told me that there's no necessity for any of those trappings. We don't have to light candles, turn cards, grasp crystals, or gaze into crystal balls to make a connection to our guides and those on the other side.

The only tools required to build and strengthen our psychic connection are an interest in connecting with our guides and an open, quiet mind.

That said, I will tell you that I sometimes enjoy lighting a candle or playing soft, instrumental music to set the mood. I've occasionally wrung a bell to clear the energy field. And, I have a lovely collection of crystals, gems, and stones on my desk. It isn't that these tools or atmosphere enhancers are required for our guides to come through to us. But, if such accoutrements help us to feel calm and comfortable, then they're worth having around. I also discovered that tarot cards helped me. In the early stages of my personal psychic development, the tarot cards helped me find language and symbols that were mutual between me and my team.

The tools I've used weren't necessary to create the connection, but at times they made me feel better, and that's what matters. We must enter into and build our psychic connection when we're open and comfortable. If having a lit candle or soft music creates a comfortable environment for you, then enjoy their presence.

Core Message #17
The Psychic Experience Should be Fun

Life should be fun. At its core and center, the reason we've reincarnated into our current physical life is because we wanted to have new, interesting, and growth-inspired experiences. And, we wanted the experience to be as enjoyable and fun as possible.

Most of our personal relationships are more enjoyable when we have fun with the other person. It's wonderful to laugh until our face and sides hurt. It's joyful to be playful together. Our relationship with those on the other side can and should be fun, too. It's just another relationship in our life. It's a relationship with others that at its foundation is based on absolute and unconditional love. What a wonderful thing to know and experience.

Yes, of course, most of us do experience challenges in life. Our hearts get broken and our feelings get hurt. Bad things do happen, and those things happen in the name of growth and experience. But, at the core of our beings the ultimate goal is to enjoy our physical lives as much as we possibly can.

Developing our psychic connection falls into that spectrum. Sure, there will be times we turn to our psychic team for guidance on difficult issues, but that's easier to do once the connection exists. The easiest way to build a strong connection with our team is to have fun in the process of doing it and then experiencing our team with love and joy.

Plus, I can tell you that most of the guides I've met, and the majority of the spirit energies I've talked to during the readings I've done for others, have involved fun loving entities. Those on the other side often have silly and fun senses of humor. They love to experience laughter and love when they connect with those of us in physical form.

Because our team of spirit guides is so fun loving, we have greater and quicker success when we approach building our psychic connection with them from an attitude of having fun on the journey. They always have laughter in their hearts, and we have a more positive experience in all aspects of our physical lives when we have laughter in our hearts as well.

Core Message #18
Our Teams Touch Us However They Can

When our psychic connection is untrained, our team of guides do whatever they can to make contact. They may come to us in dreams. We may find that we mysteriously just know a piece of information about a relationship we have with someone else. We may feel odd physical sensations that, when explored with a medical professional has no foundation or basis. They can't explain why we're physically feeling what we're feeling. Or, maybe we have a day dream or an image flashes in our mind that is interesting, fun, or helpful, but unexplainable. The best way to explain most of these types of experiences is that it's our team making contact with us.

An author friend, Terri, who recently had a suddenly psychic experience, had a strange dream that there was a white alligator under the skin on her leg. The day after the dream she had a strong physical sensation in that same spot on her leg. Terri went to see her doctor, worried that there was something physically wrong with her, but the medical professional couldn't find any cause for the painful sensation. While this was going on, she started also feeling a burning sensation on one of her fingers.

Terri and I were together a few days later at a writer's event. She didn't say anything to me about her experience, but I got a message from my team that I shared with her: "You don't need to go to the doctor for the pain."

She looked at me in amazement. "How did you know?" Terri asked.

"My team," I said. I focused and listened to my team. The message: "The sensations you're feeling are connected to the characters in your book."

Terri and I talked a bit more about her current writing project; she revealed that one of her characters had been shot in the leg and another had burned a finger during a gun battle. I received from my team that her characters, who are based on actual people who lived during and participated in the Civil War, were making a connection with her to better guide her story telling. As we talked more about the messages I was receiving, Terri experienced a wave of physical sensations throughout her body. This wave of physical feelings was the characters, and Terri's own psychic team, acknowledging and rejoicing that a connection had been strengthened.

Now, when Terri writes each day, she talks directly to her characters. Through physical sensations and other mental messages, Terri is better able to capture the feelings and emotions of her characters.

Another friend, Beth, who was a witness to the reading I shared with Terri, questioned how such painful sensations could be fun. They certainly wouldn't be fun for her. Beth had recently had a sudden psychic experience of her own, where she met a ghost who spends time in her home. I've met the ghost, whose name is Sam, while visiting Beth's home. Two pieces of jewelry had disappeared from Beth's jewelry box. She didn't think it was a thief, but didn't know what had happened to the pieces. She asked me about the jewelry during a reading. Beth had been talking about putting all her good jewelry in her bank safety deposit box. It was after that discussion that the two pieces of jewelry disappeared. I discovered that Sam had taken them, he liked them a lot and didn't want them to leave the house where he couldn't enjoy them.

Beth later told me that, after the reading, she talked frankly to Sam. She told him if he returned her jewelry she wouldn't take those pieces to the bank. The next morning she opened a dresser drawer and both pieces were sitting on top of the drawer's other contents.

Beth now sees Sam every once in a while walking through her home. She says hello to him, and they get along just fine. In fact, Beth had a flood in her home. A water pipe connection in an upstairs bathroom burst. Prior to discovering the flood, Sam was in a flurry of activity, trying to get her attention. And, the workmen who repaired the damage mentioned several times that they thought there was a ghost in the house. We discovered together that Sam had been there, keeping an eye on the progress of the workmen.

Now, to Beth, these experiences weren't difficult or painful. They actually turned out to be fun. For Terri, who has a self-proclaimed high tolerance for pain, her team took advantage of that attitude to make contact with her. Each woman now has a growing psychic connection with their own teams of spirit guides because of the experiences they had. Both find the journey they're on to be fun. Yet, if the experiences they had would be reversed, if Terri had the ghost and Beth had the pain, neither one would have enjoyed the experience.

Our teams use whatever experiences they feel will best touch us to help us discover our connection with them.

Core Message #19
Psychic Connections Can Happen at Any Time

Whether we're actively seeking them or not, our psychic awareness and connections can happen at any time. Our guides want us to find a deeper and stronger connection between us and them. They want to be of as much help to us as possible, and the best way to provide the most assistance is for us to not only accept that they exist, but to build a strong connection that we can tap into directly any time we'd like.

Discovering our psychic connection can be difficult. While our bond is always strong, our communication skills are weak. And, as we grow older and continue not to make a personal connection with our team of guides, the communication opportunities grow even weaker still.

So, when our team of guides has an opportunity to come through, when that doorway is ajar, even if just a little bit, they push through as strong as they can. After all, spirit entities are excellent opportunists. When they see the possibility, they nudge and nudge to get us into the right place at the right time. On special occasions, the results are stupendous. And, there we are, suddenly psychic.

Let me share how that happened for me...

A few weeks after my psychic encounters facilitated by Victoria Laurie, a cousin died. Christina and I were born five days apart. We celebrated many of our birthdays together, and there was always a special bond between us. While we hadn't seen each other much as adults, I continued to feel our bond. I found myself debating whether or not to attend her funeral. Funerals, after all, are for the living, not for the dead. My Uncle Jack, who had also recently died, was known for saying: "Don't come to my funeral. Come see me while I'm still alive." It didn't seem important to me to spend a lot of money to travel across the country to see my dead cousin in a box. But, something inside me kept pushing me, prodding me to attend.

I went with the strong impulse and traveled from Las Vegas, my current hometown, to northeast Ohio, where I grew up and where much of my family still lives. When I arrived in town, I had a strong desire to find Wendy, a high school friend I hadn't seen in nearly twenty years. After a bit of internet and yellow page searching, I found contact information for her sister. I visited Wendy's sister at work and found my friend. Wendy and I connected up at the place she tended bar.

After a few beers, I suddenly had a series of messages for my friend. I seemed to know things about her life that I couldn't possibly know. After all, we hadn't been in contact for decades. But, there I was sharing insights and information about her life. Poor Wendy found herself in tears. Before she headed to the restroom to clean herself up, she said: "I've needed and wanted to hear this for so long. Thank you."

One of the final things I said to her was "Now I know why I had to come to Ohio." That was a strange statement to me. Where had I recently heard that before? Of course, it was after the spontaneous psychic reading I'd received from Victoria. She said those same words to me.

As the evening with Wendy progressed, I also did a lengthy and detailed reading for her friend. Among the personal moments that we shared, I had a vision of this man kissing a baby's foot. I was embarrassed by this image and thought several moments before sharing. But, it kept appearing to me. So, I said, "I know this may sound strange, but I keep getting an image of you kissing a baby's foot."

He looked at me, shocked. "Just before I left home this evening, my three-year-old daughter stubbed her foot and was crying. I kissed it to make her feel better."

The three of us sat in disbelief. Any doubts I'd been feeling earlier about this experience being something psychic left me. There was no doubt in my mind that I'd been having a remarkable experience.

There's one final event from that evening that I want to share.

While driving around the Cleveland area tracking down Wendy, I got on the freeway. While I'd entered the correct onramp, the "Wrong Way" sign on the off ramp next to my entrance jumped out at me. It was so large, in fact, that my heart raced as if I'd entered the wrong way. I checked myself and my direction several times before I knew without doubt that I was going in the correct direction.

As I left my friend, Wendy, and her friend that evening to head back to the hotel, I felt a powerful surge of energy passing through and around me. My head was spinning and light. At the time, I chalked the feeling up to the cocktails I'd consumed.

I found my way to the freeway, waited for the turn signal, and made the left turn to enter the onramp. Once again the "Wrong Way" sign became larger than life. Only this time, I actually was going the wrong way. I was entering the freeway on the offramp, not the onramp. It was late, very dark, and the ramp was a 45 degree curve. I was too far in to back up safely. I was too far in to proceed safely forward. What to do? I thanked the universe that I'd taken out full insurance covered on the rental car and turned on my brights. I moved as far to the right in the lane as I could and inched forward. I arrived safely at US Interstate 90 to find no traffic in either direction. Not a single car or truck was traveling this major US interstate highway as far as I could see in either direction. I quickly got over my shock, turned onto the freeway, and got my car up to the speed limit.

When I arrived safe at my hotel, I logged onto the internet and begin searching for information. Something amazing had happened to me, and I wanted to understand more. I wanted to explore deeper. I knew that my life had changed, and I wanted to take advantage of the momentum. Here I was on a trip to Ohio and I was suddenly psychic.

During an early psychic channeling experience, I did readings for two of my close friends. We were together at a table when, suddenly, I started receiving messages for my friends. The messages were being shared by folks who had made their transition from their physical experiences back into source energy. The readings were fun for me and informative for my friends.

As I walked through the parking garage back to my car, I got a message for myself that I was like Lisa Williams, but different. And, that I was also like Esther Hicks, but different. I frequently received messages from my guides early on that used the "like but different" language formula.

In my early exploration of what psychics are, I came across both Lisa Williams, a psychic medium who speaks to the dead and shares their messages, and Esther Hicks who channels a group of entities known as Abraham.

Receiving that message was important and exciting to me. It felt like the first time my guides had spoken directly to me about who I was at the moment and who I was becoming as a psychic.

My experiences that night in Ohio and those in the bar, like the experiences related earlier of Beth and

Terri, were sudden psychic experiences. They were catalysts that advanced my journey of psychic awareness.

Core Message #20
It's Common to Question Sudden Psychic Experiences

Is this real or am I making it up?

One of the first questions I found myself asking about those early psychic experiences was: "Is this real or am I making it up?" It's difficult in the beginning, when initially establishing a psychic connection, to trust that we really are making a connection with spirits, angels, or entities that aren't in our physical world. It's easy and common to wonder if this is real or imaginary.

I think this question is directly connected to our early childhood. Most folks I know, when they were very young, had imaginary playmates. Over time and for varied reasons, we abandoned those playmates. Most often at the root of the abandonment was feeling or being told that our imaginary playmate experience didn't actually fit into what is considered "normal" in our society. So, we released our playmates and moved on with our lives.

I have a strong belief that for many of us, those imaginary playmates weren't make-believe at all. Instead, those playmates were our guides, angels, or even our inner self spending time with us.

As we begin to develop our psychic connection, we are once again connecting to those imaginary playmates from our earliest days. And, because we were taught as children to question the reality of those playmates, we once again question their existence.

It can be difficult, especially in the early stages of psychic connection development, to trust that our experiences with nonphysical beings are really happening. If you find yourself in that place (most of us do at some point), go ahead and play along. There's nothing wrong with make-believe. In most cases, I find that what was once make-believe becomes a strong psychic connection.

Core Message #21
Physical Sensations are a Common Form of Validation

During that early psychic reading with Victoria Laurie, when she introduced me to my grandfather, a wave of tingles passed over my body. It was a thrilling sensation that felt like a body-length hug. I didn't know it at the time, but those tingly sensations would play an important role in the development of my psychic connection.

As I began working with guided meditation, there were moments when I experienced physical sensations such as lightheadedness and tingles in my body. Some have said that the tingles are a releasing of resistance and that the lightheadedness is a raising of vibration. Based on my personal experience, there was a little more to the physical sensations.

When I directly addressed my grandfather during or just after a meditation session, I felt a physical response of tingles. It was as if he'd made a connection during that psychic reading with Victoria and was now using that sensation to continue letting me know he was there with me.

As I met each of my guides in turn, they, too, offered those physical tingles. As my connection to my team of guides grew stronger, the physical tingle sensations changed. Each of the guides, my grandfather, and my guardian angel each chose a different spot on my body to express the tingly sensation.

At this point in my psychic development, I hadn't yet developed clear language skills that allowed me to hear, see, and speak directly with my team of guides. In those first days of establishing my psychic connection, these physical sensations were a lovely form of validation that let me know I was actually talking to entities and beings outside of our physical world.

When you consider that everything in the universe is made up of energy, which explains how we can all connect, it makes sense that our guides, pure energy beings, can influence the energy around us, and that is used, to create a physical sensation.

During my early psychic development, I would occasionally get another strong sensation, almost like a subtle headache at the back of my head, just above my spine. I must admit, because I didn't understand what was happening, that there were several weeks where I took a few too many aspirin because of this physical sensation. As the headache feeling continued, I took note that it usually happened when I was in situations with other people around. When I acknowledged that fact, the feeling grew stronger, and I found myself taking more aspirin.

Over time, as my psychic language skills have improved, these physical, tingly sensations have mostly subsided. I don't have them on a regular basis anymore because my psychic connection has become stronger. Now, all I do is acknowledge my team in my mind and we can have a conversation or information exchange. But, there are still times when they offer the tingles, usually when providing support for a concept or idea or as validation of some kind. There are occasionally times that I find myself missing those tingly sensations. Not because I question my psychic connection, but because psychic hugs feel good.

As my language connection has improved between me and my team, I discovered that the lower skull headache I suffered from in public was their way of getting my attention to let me know there were messages to share with people. I've learned two things about this type of sensation. First, that it's a sign my team wants to connect with me, or second, that there's a lot of energy from transitioned spirits or entities in a small or defined space.

This discovery was wonderful to me. I knew what was causing the physical irritation. Once I understood, I was able to talk to my team about providing a better indicator, which they did. Instead of a pain sensation, I began experiencing a bit of lightheadedness. The best way I can describe the feeling is that it's like a "swoon." Another way I describe it is that it feels a little like I've had one too many cocktails, like I'm just a little drunk.

It's interesting to me though that many of the people I've provided psychic readings for have told me that they've felt tingles over their body while I'm reading them, or they find themselves feeling a little lightheaded. I take these physical sensations in others as a sign that my team is working with their team in providing the best possible psychic information during the readings, and in the process, they're also helping to raise the vibration of the person I'm reading.

When my psychic connection was in its early stages of development, the lightheadedness or dizzy feeling could be extreme at times. Here in Las Vegas, there's a major highway connection where Interstate 15 and US Highway 95 intersect. Locally, we call it the Spaghetti Bowl because of the dozens of on- and off-ramps that come together at that location. While driving through that section of freeway connections, I found myself frequently feeling extreme lightheadedness. It reached a point for awhile that I avoided the massive intersection, taking surface streets instead, so I could avoid the overwhelming feeling.

This overwhelming sensation was mirrored in other locations, too. For example, when leaving a crowded show or movie, where lots of people were entering or leaving the same location at the same time.

While this sensation doesn't feel as extreme to me anymore—I'm back to taking the freeways to travel around town—I still experience it at times. Although, now I enjoy the sensation, because I know why it's happening and what the meaning of it is.

Core Message #22
You Don't Have to Reinvent the Psychic Wheel

Each of our personal psychic journeys is unique, not only to us as we experience it, but in the universe as well. After all, the process of expanding our psychic awareness is about our personal relationship between us and our spirit guides. All relationships take time, energy, passion, and desire. There's also a bit of effort required. I resist using the word "work" to describe the effort.

At the same time, even though your relationship to your guides is a special and personal experience, and will be different from that of others in many ways, there are some similarities, too.

When I found myself to be suddenly psychic, I did what most people in our modern age would do. I headed to the internet for information and answers. I was a little surprised at how little help I found on the topic of exploring my psychic awareness. Actually, there were hundreds and hundreds of websites with information, but little of it seemed to be speaking directly to me about my sudden experience.

I spoke to a few friends about my suddenly psychic experience during my Ohio trip. One of these friends recommended I check out Lisa Williams, and someone else suggested John Edward. Another friend gave me a cassette recording of Esther Hicks and Abraham.

I have great respect for Lisa and John. Both are mediums who connect with those who have transitioned back to the energy source after a physical life experience. They share these connections with those of us who are still physical. In today's parlance, they talk to the dead. About this time, the Lifetime Network was airing Lisa Williams: Life Among the Dead which was a short television series that followed Lisa on her psychic medium routines. Not long after, I found John Edward's program on the WE Network, Cross Country. While my own reading style is quite different from both John and Lisa, there are some similarities. While watching these shows, both spoke of the symbols they received from the guides and people they spoke with on the other side. Knowing to look for symbols helped me discover symbols with my own team of guides.

Listening to Esther Hicks and Abraham had a tremendous impact on me not only as a psychic, but also my life in general. The core of Abraham's message is the Law of Attraction. Since my introduction to this material I've listened to hundreds of hours of Abraham material. I've also attended several of the live workshops. Esther Hicks and her husband, Jerry Hicks, conduct about fifty live workshop events around the country each year. And, during my own psychic and meditation work, I've had the opportunity several times to have direct contact with Abraham.

My point here is that the introduction to these materials came to me when I was searching for more information on my own psychic experience. I'm a different type of psychic than Lisa, John, and Esther. But, their experience helped and enhanced my own psychic abilities. There have also been a few others, including Max Highstein, Louise L. Hay, and Jane Roberts. If you're interested in more information on these people, visit the resource pages at the end of this book.

So, while you'll certainly develop your own psychic connection and style, it's important to know that others have traveled a similar path, and their experiences may offer some guidance or insight that will help you strengthen your own psychic connection.

Core Message #23
Psychic Connections Strengthen with Meditation

Our minds and thoughts are what drive our personal growth and expansion in all areas of our lives. It is this expansion that enhances human experience as well as expands the very source energy we all are connected to and a part of.

Yet, it is also our thoughts that can hold us back from experiencing the power and joy of life. We get so caught up in our day-to-day experience and existence, that it's easy to forget that we come from and are part of a greater source energy collective. It's difficult not to think here of the "seeing the forest for the trees" cliché. We become so focused on the little details of daily life that we sometimes forget to acknowledge and appreciate that we are part of a great forest of experience and energy. The best way to step back and acknowledge and appreciate the great forest is to take a few moments every day and meditate.

Meditation is the art and practice of quieting our mind. In our busy, technological world, we are bombarded at most turns and times with information and stimulus. This is, in itself, as we've created it. It's a good thing. But, it's also essential to step away from all that motion and activity for at least a few moments every day.

Meditation, in its most basic description, is nothing more than quieting the mind to the point of having no thoughts. For most of us, that's easier said than done. As soon as we come close to a place of a quiet mind, we quickly begin filling that quiet space with thoughts of things we could or should be doing or things that have happened to us or things that we hope to accomplish. Other common thoughts are negative self messages that we've programmed into our thought process or that have been programmed in by others, like well-meaning parents, teachers, and clergy.

When we quiet our mind, just a bit, we make room and space in our thinking to accept our place in the greater universe. There are many other benefits to meditation and quieting our mind every day that include allowing more creativity to flow to us, a greater understanding of our place and time in the universe, and, as related to our psychic connection, the ability to hear clearer the messages being shared by our spirit guides.

There are many different forms and types of meditation. For example, you may have heard of Transcendental Meditation (TM), especially if you are a Beatles fan. There are also active meditation techniques (like TM, where you utilize a mantra or other repeated words or phrases), passive techniques, living in the now techniques...the list goes on and on. All of the different meditation techniques work if they help you accomplish a quiet mind in the process of performing them.

There are so many techniques of achieving the goal of a quiet mind through meditation that I can't give you a "best" or "perfect" way. What I can tell you is that the main goal of meditation is plain and simple: relax and quiet your mind for at least 10-15 minutes each day. I can also tell you that there is absolutely no wrong way to go about meditating. My own meditation style has changed over time, and I expect it will change many more times as I continue my current journey. Through experimentation you will discover the best method for you at this moment.

There are three types of meditation I use: Quiet Mind, Guided, Psychic.

In Quiet Mind Meditation, I release all thought, breath deeply, and relax. Guided Meditation has helped me meet my guides and expand my psychic connection. Psychic Meditation is the time I spend with my team of spirit guides, teachers, and angels.

Quiet Mind Meditation

I first get into a comfortable sitting position. (Every time I try to meditate while lying down flat on my back, I fall asleep. While relaxation is a prime goal of meditation, sleeping is not.) I sit comfortably, eyes closed, with my arms at my side. I take several deep breaths and feel myself sink a little deeper into my chair. For the next ten minutes or so, I keep breathing deeply. As any thought enters my mind, I release it with the thought: "this thought isn't necessary at this moment." If it's an important thought or idea, I ask, silently in my mind, that the important thought be remembered later. I keep breathing and releasing any thought that flits through. I often find myself "seeing" a blank, black space. After my quiet mind meditation, I slowly open my eyes and resume my day. That's it.

I sometimes play soft background music while I meditate. I find some instrumental music is helpful to block out street noise and other sounds. Using the same music over and over in the background during my meditation time also acts like a timer for my meditation sessions. For an excellent selection of meditation CDs, visit www.SerenityMusic.com.

One tip: Don't set any type of alarm. It's important to not startle yourself out of your quiet state or to deteriorate your meditation by anticipating the sound of an alarm.

Guided Meditation

One of the most helpful tools I discovered for expanding my psychic connection was guided meditation. Guided meditation is just that, a guided experience. There are several ways to experience this. One method is to take advantage of guided meditation recordings created by others. Another method is to create a recording of your own voice that follows a script and guides you during meditation.

How it works: The recording, usually a quiet, supportive voice speaks above quiet background music and offers thoughts and suggestions that guide your meditation experience. It's kind of like a meditation "how to." I've used the guided meditation recordings from Lisa Williams and Max Highstein to great success. Their recordings have helped me meet my spirit guides, my angel, and open up, build, and strengthen my psychic connection.

I started with a 16-lesson course centered on guided meditation called Intuition Retreat from Max Highstein. It's offered in a combination of book and CD form. As I began working Max's guided meditation course, I had some wonderful experiences connecting with my inner self and meeting my spirit guides. These early meetings and messages were choppy and bumpy, but along the way, Max's kind, gentle voice supported me on my journey. I had incredible success with Max's course and highly recommend it.

One of Max's guided meditations involves meeting and getting to know our inner self. Some refer to this as our inner child, while others explain that our inner self or inner being is the part of us that remains nonphysical, in source energy. During a guided meditation when I met my inner self, I was given a strong image of a white tiger.

Living in Las Vegas, we have zoo-like access to Siegfried and Roy's famous white tigers via their Secret Garden at the Mirage. I put off visiting there for a bit, still not believing that the psychic experiences I was having were actually real. But, I eventually made my way over to the Secret Garden. I wandered around the little zoo and enjoyed seeing the animals. Then, I noticed a crowd standing around a small, windowed building. Like a lemming, I joined the crowd to see what they were looking at. There, through the glass, was a litter of baby tigers romping and playing with their handler. A chill ran down my entire body and the tingles continued for several moments. I knew at that moment that I wasn't making up my psychic connection in my mind. I knew, without a doubt, that my inner self and spirit guides used the tiger message to validate my recent psychic experiences. I visited the gift shop at the conclusion of my visit and purchased a stuffed white tiger. He now looks down on me from my bookshelf, a talisman of this personal psychic breakthrough experience.

After Max's course, I discovered Lisa Williams' guided mediation recordings. Like Max, Lisa takes you on a personal journey to help open and expand your psychic connection.

I had a lovely experience with my angel, Michael, during a Lisa Williams guided meditation. As we were talking to each other, Lisa's guided meditation came back and we were interrupted. How annoying I found it. Now, I laugh about it though. If it hadn't been for the guided meditation I might have had a longer time journey in meeting Michael. But, now that I'd met him, I felt annoyed by the interruption of the voice on the recording. Don't get me wrong, I adore and appreciate Lisa Williams. But, yes, I was also annoyed.

Michael was loving and told me that we could meet

again and speak again, as often as I wanted without the guided CD.

Psychic Meditation

After the experience with Michael and Lisa Williams' guided meditation, I spent some time figuring out my own psychic meditation technique. This, like the quiet meditation, has changed over time. I begin the same way as my quiet mind meditation, sitting comfortably, breathing deeply, and relaxing. Sometimes, I have background music, and sometimes I don't. I quiet my mind to that blank, black slate, and I call on Michael (or other members of my psychic team). In that quiet place we talk.

In the very beginning, I'd sometimes hear them, sometimes feel them, and sometimes see them. As my skills and abilities improved, as my psychic connection grew stronger, I began hearing, seeing, and feeling all at the same time. My team has answered questions, shared information, and supported me in more general ways.

My psychic meditation has now evolved to a place that I don't require any music or even long relaxation to hear, see, and feel them. Instead, in the literal blink of an eye, I connect with my team and chat with them. They're just there with me when I want them.

Core Message #24
Symbolism and Language Enhance Psychic Communication

Once a psychic connection is established, we require a way to communicate with our team of guides. Some who find themselves suddenly psychic will also discover they have a deep immediate connection and can communicate easily with their team. Others, like me, will want to develop their communication skills.

Learning to communicate with your team can be like learning a foreign language. And, there are many ways to go about this learning process.

My team has been very clear over the years that no special tools are required, yet I'm about to talk about using some different tools to enhance your language skills with your own team. The bottom line is that you don't actually have to have any special tools to strengthen your connection to team. Over time, through meditation, you will discover and develop your personal methods of communication. Personally, I became a little impatient during that phase of my own psychic development. I wanted stronger communication skills as quickly as possible. I was so excited to discover my spirit guides and wanted to talk to them and understand them.

One way to think about this is like your own reading skills. Today, you can read any book in your own language. You don't even think about it when you read the words on a sign or billboard. Now, think back to when you first learned how to read. If you're like most of us, you learned each letter and the sound of that letter. You next were taught how to form those letters into small, known words like "dog" or "cat." The words started getting larger and you had vocabulary lists to learn. You became familiar with the dictionary and frustrated at times, because you couldn't find a word, because you didn't know how to spell it. Maybe, along the journey, you used flash cards and had others quiz you. Yet today, you don't even think about those early experiences when you pick up the latest novel by your favorite author. You simply open the cover and read. And even today, when you run across a word you don't know, you head to a dictionary to discover its meaning.

Developing your psychic language skills is a similar journey to learning how to read words on a page. Sure, you can just keep stabbing at the language, hoping you'll understand the meaning, or you can do a few exercises that will strengthen your communication knowledge.

It's a little funny now, to make the extended connection, but I used a deck of tarot cards, rather like flashcards, to expand my language and symbol knowledge.

I'd felt drawn to tarot cards about a year or so before my psychic channels opened. I've had tarot readings several times and decided to include a series of readings in a novel I was writing. It was fun to look at the pictures, but at that point, I didn't take the time to learn what the cards meant. Instead, I turned to a few of my tarot reading friends and asked them to help me create readings for the hero in my story.

After my psychic connections began to open, I had trouble understanding the early messages. I knew my team was there, they were giving me lots of physical sensations at that point. But, language was still a problem between us.

For some reason I didn't understand at the time, I was once again drawn to the tarot cards. I learned a few tarot spreads (the way the cards are placed in certain positions for readings) and proceeded to begin turning cards and checking in the little book I had what the cards' meanings were. I'll admit, in those early days, I had trouble keeping track of everything that came up. After all, looking at a card, turning to the book, reading the meaning, moving on to the next card, etc. was difficult. So, I started taking notes in shorthand about the card meanings.

I also have to admit that I still don't know all the card meanings, even after several years. I began to trust and understand that the tarot wasn't going to be at the core of my communication method.

What did start to happen, as I took page after page of notes, is that I found myself with a strong desire to free write after my tarot spread session. Being a writer, putting words on paper is natural to me.

What I discovered over time was that I was correct that the cards wouldn't become important to me as a method of reading for myself or others, but they did provide a series of shorthand symbols. They provided a starting place of common language between me and my guides.

One of the first strong messages I got while using the combination of tarot cards and free writing included: Sedona vortex, trees with a view, and pot.

I was a little surprised about the pot reference. During my musician days, I did enjoy getting stoned on occasion, but it had been years since I'd partaken in smoking marijuana. But, the guides said it, and I figured there might be some special experience that would come about because of the drug enhanced state.

We've all read stories of drug induced states in Native American culture and the counter culture of the 1960s. So, I talked to a few friends, and within six degrees of separation I found a theater friend with a pot connection.

I felt excited about getting stoned. It'd been so long. One afternoon I smoked some of the pot and waited for something special to happen. While it was fun to experience the feeling brought on by the drug, I didn't have any kind of awakening or discover a deeper connection with my team. I admit, I felt a little disappointed.

A short time later, I got in the car and drove to

Sedona. I love to drive and enjoyed the mountains and views of the area. I arrived in Sedona, found one of the vortex areas, and began walking around. I'd brought my notebook. I was ready for something special to happen. I wandered and wandered through a field until I found a group of trees with a view of the Sedona valley. Through physical sensations, my team let me know I was in the correct place. It was lovely, but no special messages came. I again felt disappointed.

When I looked down, there, next to the trees with a view, were several bushes with seed pods hanging on them. The word, it turns out, wasn't "pot" but rather "pod." That made me chuckle and via physical sensations, I could feel my team enjoying the moment, too.

I found a spot on a small boulder with a nice vantage of the sunset. While waiting for the sun to descend, I opened my note book and waited, just in case. Nothing happened. I asked them in my head, why did you bring me here if nothing special was going to happen? That's when their message came. They said very clearly in my head: "You were able to understand us enough for you to leave your home, travel for many hours to a place you've never been before, and find a group of trees. That is important. That is special. It validates that you can understand us now."

Well, there I sat on that rock, tears streaming down my face, while a wave of excitement came over me. It's true. I did understand them. I'd validated my understanding by going to a new place and having them confirm that in fact I'd done exactly the correct thing.

Are you familiar with the story of Helen Keller? Helen was a deaf mute child born in America in the nineteenth century. Her parents believed, as was the custom of that time, that Helen, because of her physical ailments of being both deaf and blind, was unreachable and therefore unteachable. They called on Annie Sullivan to be a caregiver for Helen. Annie believed that Helen was teachable. After weeks and weeks of teaching, teaching that Helen didn't understand, the family was about to give up when Helen experienced a small connection between the sign language Annie was trying to teach and the knowledge of what water was. Helen made the connection. There was a sudden leap between something known (water) and something previously unknown (sign language). That small connection led Helen to become one of America's great personalities. She wrote articles and books and toured the American lecture circuit for many years.

I believe all new psychics go through a similar moment at some point when building their psychic connection. We work and work, often to the point of frustration, as we attempt to establish some type of communication system between us and our spirit guides. Then, with barely the blink of an eye, we have a moment of connection, a moment where all the pieces of the puzzle fall into place and we can understand the messages being shared by our team.

While tools such as tarot cards, music, candles, and incense might not be required to establish a psychic connection, they are sometimes aids in helping us find a connection with our spirit guides.

Core Message #25
Surprise Connections with Strangers Happen

Your psychic connection may grow in a trickle or a raging waterfall. There's no way to determine in advance how it will expand. What I have learned is that the more experience you gain in establishing contact and communicating with your team the easier our psychic connections happen.

The readings I did in Ohio early on my psychic journey happened without my trying to "make" them happen. Frankly, my team saw an opportunity and took advantage of it. They took advantage of similar openings a few months later.

When I was well into working through Max's intuition course, I met some friends one evening. We were talking about my experiences when, suddenly, I could see dead people. As we talked, a guy who had transitioned from physical came through. As I relayed the messages I received to my friend, we discovered that the dead guy was a close friend of hers who had died under strange circumstances. The dead guy offered answers to some of her questions and also mentioned a note he'd left behind. My friend was able to confirm later that there was, in fact, a note and, up until my reading, the dead guy's daughter was the only person who knew about it.

Not to be left out, the late husband of my other friend came through that evening. He didn't have much to say, but showed me his mannerisms and offered a few key phrases. I'd never met this man when he was living a physical life and my friend who had been married to him never talked about him. It was an amazing evening. And, while I did have doubts at the time of the surprise readings, wondering whether the experiences I was having were real or not, the friends who received the information were able to provide validation that the information I shared, that I couldn't have known, was honest information.

Bolstered by my experiences I continued my journey into psychic awareness. I'd been working with the different forms of meditation for a few months. After I'd worked my way through Max's intuition course and guided meditations. I was open to the experience of connecting with my team and having fun with it. I found myself meeting new people who also had sudden psychic experiences, including my friend Sara Wiseman. Sara is psychic and the author of Writing to the Divine: How to Use Channeling for Soul Growth & Healing.

While speaking at a writer's conference in the Northwest, Sara and I met for dinner. As we enjoyed a good meal, we talked about our own psychic experiences and growth. Without warning, I found myself seeing and talking to her father who had transitioned from physical some time ago. I shared the messages I received. I was also able to answer questions that Sara had about her dad. It was the first time I experienced my clairsentient ability. I could feel Sara's dad's heartfelt emotion, and as I shared his messages, I found myself with an overwhelming feeling of love and also had tears in my eyes. As quickly as this psychic experience came, it ended.

Later that same weekend, after presenting my session for the writers, I was at the hotel bar enjoying a beer. The space was filled with people, most of them writers attending the conference. There's a lovely energy that grows and builds during weekend writer events. Most writers spend a lot of time in isolation, so when you gather them together, they're excited to have others to talk to, learn from, and share with. In addition, many writers who attend these events are attempting to pitch and sell their works to the agents and publishers who are also there. Let me tell you, whether you're psychic or not, it's easy to feel all the energy that swirls around.

As I enjoyed my drink and felt all this energy I experienced an overwhelming swirl of energy, like a swoon. At first, I thought the local brewery drink might have a very high alcohol content. But then, I felt the presence of an older woman. I was compelled to speak to the woman sitting next to me. This was my first reading for an absolute stranger. I hesitated to say anything at first. How strange was this? But, the sensational feeling I was experiencing grew stronger and stronger until I felt I had no choice but to speak.

I leaned toward the woman and said, "Do you believe in psychics?" She was a bit taken aback at my question, but smiled and told me she did believe in them. "Well," I said, "I know this is going to sound strange, but I've got a woman here who wants to talk to you." The eyes of the lady next to me grew large. For the next 15 or 20 minutes, I shared the information I received, and the lady validated much of what I said about weddings, births, and a future party her family was planning.

The psychic readings that weekend, along with several of the people I met who also had strong, new psychic abilities, were incredible. I hadn't planned for any of this. I was attending the conference as a speaker on the topic of internet self promotion for writers, not as a psychic.

As you open your psychic channel and strengthen your psychic connections. anything really is possible. Your team will take positive advantage of the situations you're in to come through to you. This will enhance your own psychic journey and experience and will also provide a strong level of validation that, yes, this psychic thing is not only real, but it's happening to you.

On another occasion during this same period of time, I was visiting a local gallery. The show was a collection of great American painters. I wandered the gallery alone. There weren't any other visitors in the small rooms. I'd attended the show because there were several paintings on display by Georgia O'Keeffe. For as long as I can remember I've felt a connection to and fondness for Georgia's work. I do love the big, bright, bold paintings of flowers and Southwest landscapes. But, I also really enjoy her other, earlier works of darker cityscapes. As I was enjoying the paintings, I could hear a voice in my head. I knew it wasn't my own, and I also knew that it didn't sound like my team of guides. I listened harder and knew it was Georgia speaking to me. She actually took me into one of her paintings and explained what was behind the adobe wall that she had created on the canvas. The whole experience was surreal. I enjoyed it thoroughly, but couldn't help wondering afterward if it had actually happened, if it had been "real."

I embrace these experiences. They excite and enchant me. I think that because I enjoy them so much that more and more experiences have opened for me. And, with each reading I perform and each psychic meditation session I experience, my connection with my team grows stronger.

Core Message #26
Validation is all Around Us

As we expand and strengthen our psychic connections the question again comes up: "Am I making all this up?" The way to discover that our psychic connections are real is through validation, or proof that the information shared is solid and real.

From the very beginning of my psychic connection, my team has offered me validation in different forms. I've learned information I couldn't have known. I've seen images of people I've never met, but when I describe them to others, they know exactly who I'm talking about. During readings for others, I've been given key phrases that someone always used to say. And, on a more personal level, there were my experiences with the white tiger cubs and Sedona.

During a reading, I received the message: "Ask about when she was nineteen and who Jimmy or John was." The woman I was providing a reading for gasped. "John was my first husband," she exclaimed. "I never talk about him. He made my life miserable." I questioned her further about the age of nineteen. "I was nineteen when we met," she said. There was no way I could have known about John or that she met him when she was 19-years-old.

One of my favorite experiences was when I first started offering phone readings. As I read for a woman who was a friend of friend, someone I'd never before talked to, I suddenly had an image of a house in my head. I talked, describing where the rooms were and how the furniture was placed. At the end of the tour I asked the woman if this place made any sense or had any meaning. She told me I'd just toured her house. We were both quite amazed at the experience.

Validation from our team comes in vast and varied ways. It might be as simple as having a feeling that you want to drive a different way home from work. You don't know why, but have a strong feeling to go a different way. Then, the next morning you read in the paper about a car accident that you avoided by not going your usual way. Or, validation might come in bigger ways, like being told by your team of guides that the book you're looking for is the third one in on the second shelf of a bookstore you've never visited before.

As a professional psychic, I love when clients offer validation. It's an absolute sign that we were very well connected during our reading time. I had a client who was virtually silent during our reading time. Without any in-the-moment validation, I didn't know for sure if the information I'd shared was correct or if it had any positive impact. A few days later I received an email from that client telling me that the reason they were so quiet and silent was, at first, because they didn't want to give up any information, but as the reading progressed, they couldn't believe how accurate my words were.

However you receive validation, take it as a sign that your team is there for you, helping you navigate your life journey experience.

Core Message #27
Our Guides Have a Great Sense of Humor

Being happy is really what our lives are supposed to be about. As in all other aspects of our life journey, our guides are here to help us. They love when we're happy and they love to help us find ways to be happier. Of course, laughter is the fastest way to arrive at a feeling of happiness. I'm constantly amazed at the great sense of humor our guides have. They love to laugh and to laugh along with us on our journey.

Once I connected with my team, I frequently heard them laughing in my ear. They don't laugh at us, they laugh with us. After all, their whole job in interacting with us is to guide our journey toward a positive experience. They in no way want to make us feel bad or self-conscious for any reason. They want to do what they can to help lighten our experience to a positive place. By helping us understand better how to lift the weight off our own shoulders, they help us raise our vibrational state of being.

Finding more ways to enjoy our life, to laugh, and

have fun has a positive effect on our life journey. When we smile and laugh, whether alone or with others, we raise our vibration to a higher state. This raising of our vibration brings us closer to them and more in tune with source energy. When we're closer to them, it's also easier to utilize our psychic connection.

When we're happy, when we go through life laughing and loving, we're less likely to have negative experiences. When we spend our time in laughter and enjoyment, we're less likely to suffer physical ailments. Positive energy is good for us, and laughter and lightheartedness are outward and inward expressions of that positive life experience.

Our guides not only support us, they also lead us by example. I love to hear them chuckle in my ear. I love to connect with those who have transitioned and feel the love that flows through them to us. Even when the messages from those on the other side are of a serious nature, they provide those messages from a place of love.

Because we create our own experience, it makes sense that we take on the goal of creating positive, loving experiences. Because the goal of physical life is joy and happiness, it makes sense that we do what we can to attain them. And, because laughter is the quickest way to raise our vibration into a light and positive place, it makes sense that our guides are already in that state and lead us there by example.

Lighten up. Laugh more. Love more.

Core Message #28
All We Have is Now and the Future

I'll admit, I do have an overall tendency to take life too seriously. I think many of us humans have that trait ingrained in us from very young ages. We worry too much. We over-think most situations. Instead of living in the moment, we tend to rehash the past over and over, trapping us into a belief that those past patterns are our life patterns.

A great discovery for me was that, when working with my team of guides, I have to be in the moment. They've helped me work through some of my past emotional issues, but I do believe that the undercurrent of the time I spend with my team is about being in this moment and looking not at the past, but at the future. This makes sense. We can't alter or change the past. It's done. All we can do with it is learn from the moments we've already lived and move on toward the future. The role of our guides is to help us navigate our way in a loved and positive way into the future that we want and desire. Since we're here and headed into the future, it makes sense to move through our physical time in a joyous, comfortable, and fun-loving way.

Most of us carry the baggage of our lives. The older we get, the more baggage we acquire to carry around. The past, instead of becoming a learning experience, becomes a baggage terminal where we keep claiming all the hurts, hardships, and negative experiences we've lived through.

Our past experiences are important, and I don't want to say they're not. They've helped us learn and grow and become the person we are today. Those experiences along our journey also shape the person we are and will be long past this current life experience. We maintain our individual personalities after we transition from physical life, and it stands to reason that the experiences we've had have a very long-term purpose for us.

The baggage we carry isn't past experience, but rather the emotions we experienced as we journeyed through those times. We don't desperately cling to the positive experiences. Instead, it's negative emotions that hold our attention and time. What's most important is that we let go of the emotions of those past experiences and only retain the knowledge of the experience.

There's also an age-old adage that those who don't learn history are doomed to repeat it. I can tell you that this is a false concept. In fact, because of the Law of Attraction, we're more likely to repeat the past when we know about and study it.

Learning to live in the moment and look forward toward the future is probably one of the most difficult things I've had to learn to do. I don't know that we can ever gain perfection at it, but it is worth trying to accomplish. We can never change the past. It's done and complete, unchangeable, no matter how many times we think it through and wish it were different. So, why bother reliving it and rethinking it over and over? It's just a waste of our precious time and energy.

Your past has served its purpose. It's gotten you to where you are today. Whether you feel positive or negative at this moment about your past experiences is basically irrelevant. All that matters is that you use your current point to move toward your future direction.

Now, I'm not saying that we should start from scratch each day. How horrible would it be if we had to start each day learning once again how to read and write? No, it's good to bring the knowledge and learning from our past forward into this moment. What we want to release and let go of are the negative emotions we experienced along our life's journey. Remember how to read and write, but if you had a horrible writing teacher who wrapped your knuckles each time you got an answer wrong and every time you think about it you feel negative emotion, that's the piece of your life puzzle you'll want to let go of.

Our time and energy are so much better spent living in the moment and looking forward to the future that we want. As you grow your psychic connection, you'll quickly discover that your team won't help you spend time on the past. They won't spend time analyzing your life experience in great detail unless there's a direct correlation to where you are at the moment and where you are heading in your future.

Embrace the joy of life in the now. Embrace the love that our guides and angels always feel toward us and share with us. In embracing those realities, it's difficult if not impossible not to feel good. And, when we feel good and live life through laughter, joy, and love, we glide in an easier fashion through our time.

Learn from the past, release emotion, live in the moment, and dream about a positive future.

Core Message #29
There is a Reason for Every Psychic Message

When first developing and strengthening your psychic connection, the messages you receive may seem simple, small, and even unimportant. As I discussed earlier, some of my first messages were about little things like the local tigers and nearby physical locations. Some of the first dead folks I saw and heard didn't seem to have much to say. Even now, after hundreds and hundreds of psychic readings, I sometimes have a dead person who comes through during a reading, and they don't have much if anything to say beyond "I'm fine" or "I love you."

In my early psychic development, I felt that everything that happened was important. Yet, when the end results, like a simple "I love you" message, didn't have the great answers of the universe attached, I felt disappointed.

I can tell you now that even those simple little messages are important. During your early psychic connection development, as you're just beginning to develop the language and symbol skills between you and your team, those little messages are important. They are building your connection with your team of spirit guides and providing small examples of validation that the connection you're building is real. As your connection grows stronger and your ability to interpret images, words, sounds, and feelings shared by your spirit guides improves, some messages will be more profound. Some, though, will remain simple and "unimpressive."

Just because we build and grow our connection doesn't mean that we'll be receiving answers to all the great questions of the universe. Sometimes, dead folks just want to say hello and let you know they're okay and that they love you.

One of my favorite discoveries happened when I started to offer psychic readings for others. Many of the messages I received for other people also helped me better understand myself. Some messages for others answered questions that I had in my own life. One of the discoveries from this experience was that we are all, every single person living today on the planet and all the other people who have ever lived on the planet, are all connected energetically. While our personal experiences are our own, they are also part of the collective human experience.

We must also be conscious that a message that may seem insignificant to us as we receive it may be incredibly important to someone else. While doing a client reading, I got the image of a white, men's tube sock. Such a strange and small message. I was hesitant to share it. Yet, that image kept coming to me, so I finally did share it with the client. That simple image turned out to have significant meaning because it was related to his wife and her business. It was a validation not only that I was connected to source energy information, but also validation of a discussion the client and his wife had been having earlier that week.

So often, little messages that don't seem or feel important at the time we receive them hold importance and meaning later. It may be days, weeks, or even months after a little message that we get our "aha" moment about the message. Listen, see, hear, and feel all that your team offers you. They wouldn't take the time and energy necessary to share a message if they didn't know that it held an important meaning for you.

Core Message #30
The Goal is to Gain Information and Insight

There's a common belief among many of the psychics I've met that psychics can't read very well for themselves. This is something I disagree with. The best use and goal of our psychic connection is to help us better guide our own lives. The main task of our spirit guides is to aid and assist us in all that we do. They provide this assistance whether we're conscious of their presence or not. That's the agreement we made with our spirit guides before we came into our physical form.

Where the confusion about not being able to read well for ourselves comes from is that sometimes it's easier to hear a message given through another than to hear it when given directly. It's so often easier to give advice rather than take advice. Sometimes, for many different reasons, we aren't willing to hear the advice directly from our team, but when it comes through another psychic, we can hear it better. It's out in the open as it were. This is one of the reasons that many people with psychic gifts and abilities will "swap" readings.

I believe the ultimate goal of our psychic abilities is to use them to guide our direction in life. When we have choices to make or when we face forks in the road, our team is happy to help us figure out what decisions will best help us attain what we most want in life.

It's fun to note that our teams won't always share the answers with us. They won't always predict event outcomes or our future. The reason we came into physical form was for the experience of living, with all the joy and pain the human experience involves. In the long run, it's of no benefit for us to have all the answers so that our life here on Earth is easy all the time.

There are times when I meet with my team during psychic meditation because I want to figure out an issue I'm experiencing. I want to understand clearer where I am and where I'm heading. My team will offer some help and guidance and, now that I've built a rather positive connection with my team, they'll jokingly chide me that they can't share that information. Sometimes, they won't share information because it's just not time (I have a tendency to want to be way forward in my life journey before I've gone through the steps or experiences to get me to that point). There are also times when I'm curious about some facet of the spiritual world. I want to know how the universe works with more detail than I currently know. And, there are moments during such explorations where they offer that they can't explain it to me because there are no words or references that could possibly explain how that aspect of the universe works. In those moments though, they do offer that when I arrive back in spirit form, when my time in the physical realm is completed, that I'll once again have full knowledge of how the universe works.

Just because we want to know an answer or a piece of information doesn't mean that our team will give it to us. Sometimes, we're not ready for that knowledge. At other times, the knowledge we seek is irrelevant to the moment. There are also times when having the knowledge we seek may disrupt the learning and lessons that will happen. Our team of guides is always looking out for our best interests so we have to trust them to share information and knowledge when it's best for us, not just because we want it.

Core Message #31
Reading for Others Strengthens Your Psychic Connection

Giving psychic readings to others strengthens our psychic abilities. Because we're reading for someone else, it's often easier to hear the messages and share the information. There's also the added benefit of receiving additional validation because the person you read for can let you know if the information you're providing is valid or not, or if the predictions for their future come true or not. Between the additional validation and the additional experience of building your language skills between you and your team, you'll strengthen even more your psychic connection. This stronger connection will also help you hear messages for yourself with greater clarity in the future. So, the experience turns out as a win-win for everyone involved.

Another interesting occurrence when we read for others is that parallels often appear between the messages that are offered for the person you are reading for and yourself. Frequently, the messages I receive for my clients hold a deep relevance for me as well. Again, this is a way that our teams work together to gently nudge us into a greater understanding of our own life experiences.

I have been truly blessed throughout my psychic journey with a group of very good friends who have allowed themselves and even offered themselves to be my psychic reading "guinea pigs." They've allowed me to do psychic readings and tarot readings which have certainly helped me to develop, expand, strengthen, and deepen my own psychic connection. I have been pleasantly surprised over and over by my friends' willingness to go along with me on my journey. They've also been supportive in various other ways, as very good friends are.

Once you're feeling ready, find a friend who is willing to be a "guinea pig" for you. Ask them if they'd be willing to help you play with your ever growing psychic skill. Hopefully, you'll be as pleasantly surprised that you will have willing friends.

Just as there's no one way to be psychic and not everyone uses the same psychic methods, there's no one way to perform a psychic reading for yourself or for others. As with so many experiences in life, it's trial by fire. We just have to dive in and try it, see what works, hold on to those things, and release the methods and attempts that don't produce positive results.

At first, I copied the methods of the psychics I knew, the ones I'd had readings from. I also copied some of the methods I'd seen psychics on television programs use. Many of the early readings I performed were bumpy. It sometimes felt like I was groping for information. Then, because I wasn't confident about the information, I didn't know if I was truly sharing psychic messages or just making stuff up. In many of my early readings, it turned out to be a bit of both. What I discovered though is that frequently the stuff I thought I was making up was not actually fantasy, but rather me incorrectly interpreting the messages, images, and information I was actually receiving from my team.

One of the important things I learned during those early readings was to simply trust the information I was getting. If something came to me, I had to share it as I got it instead of trying to filter it in some way. Sometimes, the words came out backwards or jumbled, but still, I just shared what I got. From the professional psychics I've talked to, that's a common lesson for just about all of them: Learning to let go of our personal filters and just sharing the information and images as they come. Talk through it, don't think about it.

Core Message #32
Sometimes Message Receivers Become the Messengers

During a phone reading, a dead guy came through. It took us a while to figure out that he was the father of the client's daughter-in-law, a young woman the client didn't have a positive relationship with. To top it off, the dead father wanted the client to share a message with his daughter, a task the client wasn't happy being asked to do.

At first, I thought messages like this were simply the dead folk taking advantage of the open channel. But, there's more to it than that. I talked to my team about this experience and asked them why it happens. They told me that, while often these messages appear to be for another person, there's an important reason why they come through when they do. It's usually not just the dead person taking advantage of the experience, although this can happen. Like the day Jose's grandmother came through during a phone reading, and it turned out Jose was a gardener working outside on the opposite side of my office wall. Instead, there's a reason that the message shared with one person will be given by that person to someone else. There's something about their relationship with this person that will be enhanced or strengthened because of the message sharing.

This concept makes sense. After all, most of the readings I do end up benefiting me as well as the person I'm reading for. Sometimes, it's because I receive new symbols or stories to use in the future. Sometimes, the reading provides a new experience, like helping me learn a new ability or skill. Frequently, when the messages become a little emotional, there is some personal learning that is paralleled between the person receiving the reading and my own life and experience.

Whenever energy beings come together and share information and experience, we all tend to learn from one another. Even more important, when those on the other side come through with a message, there's always an important reason why that message was shared at that moment, even if it appears to be just a little thing or a message for someone not even there at the moment.

In the case of my client, she shared the messages we received with her daughter-in-law and discovered they both are interested in spirits and energy beings. Because the message was shared, the two now have a more positive relationship.

Core Message #33
Symbols Come in Many Forms

I like to think of symbols as a way for our psychic team to deliver lots of information in a type of shorthand. Many psychics enjoy this shorthand.

The nice thing about psychic symbols is that they convey lots of information in a single thought or image. When the same symbols recur again and again over time, they also serve a function as information validators.

Psychic symbols are different for almost everyone. As you develop your own psychic connection and language skills, you'll begin to discover your own set of symbols. Here are two that developed for me.

The Life Path

While I truly believe there is no predestined goal or end for any of us, I do believe that each of us is on a life journey. Each of us is on a life path. My team shows me this as a path that stretches out ahead of where we are.

There is only one pre-determined life experience for each of us. That is, when we leave our physical bodies, we will return fully to source energy. So, this concept gives a destination for our path. What is not pre-determined is what our experiences will be along that path. One point of clarity is that we do arrive in physical as babies having chosen our parents and the early life experiences they will provide for us.

Once the symbol was set for me (the life path), my team could then start giving me additional images that added to the meaning and depth of the message; for example, forks, trees, mountains, etc.

As we journey through life, each of us enjoy many forks in our paths. Sometimes, when performing readings, I'll see a fork that leads to parallel paths, each rejoining the main path. Other forks lead into forests or trees, around mountains, traversing great distances.

Because of free will, we may choose any of the forks we desire. There is no "right" or "wrong" path, ever. Although, different paths and forks will provide different experiences, some more challenging than others.

When someone asks me about their future, my team shows me the life path symbol. They then proceed to show me forks, choices, and possible challenges. Through these symbols and images, I'm often able to share what is coming up for someone in the near-term. Sometimes, I can also see long-term events, but because of free will and the Law of Attraction, the long term can easily be changed by near-term choices.

One of my favorite life path symbols are forks. I sometimes see not a single fork, but many. This is an indication that the person has many possible directions they can follow. Sometimes, if there are lots of possibilities, the forks stretch out like dozens of fingers, each pointing in a new direction.

The Arc of Personal Experience

Searching for my purpose and passion in life, I've had a recurring tendency to take on lots and lots of projects. I like to try things. What starts to happen though is that I develop a new idea or project; I'm excited about its possibilities, but then, discover the project isn't providing the inspiration or passion that I'd hoped for. So, I'd move on to a new project. Instead of letting go of the old project, I'd keep that one going, too. Soon, I'm attempting to juggle many balls at the same time, none of them creating the desired passion, and after a time, they don't even provide much interest. But, out of a sense of obligation, I try to keep them all going.

My team helped me better understand what was happening with an Arc of Personal Experience symbol. They showed me a half circle. Along the line there were little dots, each representing a different project or creative endeavor. They then asked me to focus in my mind on any one of the project dots. As I focused on the dot, it spread out like an ink blot. The more I focused on it, the bigger the ink stain grew.

As I pulled my focus back, that growing spot reduced back to a small dot on the arc. Next, they told me to focus on a different dot. Again, as I focused, that dot grew into a larger and larger ink blot.

My team explained that there's nothing wrong with having lots of dots on my arc. Most of us have lots of dots. They also asked what was most important to me. I told them that I want to feel passion and excitement about something in my life. I want to apply my time and energy to something that I enjoy and that brings me joy. And, I want the biggest life I can possibly have.

Based on my response, my team showed me that the goal then isn't having a lot of things going on at all times, but rather having something we enjoy doing and intensely focusing on that idea or project.

I asked: how can we just let go of all those other things? There are people who have come to desire and even depend on those other projects.

My team responded with a wonderful truth: We are all on a personal journey. We have no actual responsibility to anyone else, not if it means we give up our own power and desire to serve another. Instead, our only responsibility is to ourselves and to our own personal journey. In the process of stepping away from a project or endeavor, we not only are serving our own desires and journey, but we are also providing experience to others around us.

Yes, this may appear selfish, and for someone like me, raised with a strong Midwest work ethic that comes with a commitment to others—if we say we'll do something we must do it whether we want to or not—it's been one of the most difficult concepts for me to understand and embrace.

As I stepped away from many different time-consuming and wheel-spinning projects, I discovered that the world would not end. Yes, there were some in my life who expressed disappointment, but that disappointment I discovered was their issue, not my issue. As I let go of project after project, I had time to focus on fewer things. My attention wasn't split, and the little dots on my arc, now fewer, were easier to focus on and allow to grow.

Another thing I've learned from this Arc of Personal Experience symbol is that at any point, when I'm done focusing on something, I can step away from it and focus on something else as I desire.

In addition to symbols that come through as images in my mind's eye, my team also now uses shorthand for sharing information through stories. Sometimes, they'll express to me: "share the story of free will," or "share the message about dead relatives and friends." When I get those prompts from my team of spirit guides, I share the related information in greater detail with my those I'm reading for based on previous, longer messages that I've received. As you develop your psychic connection, you'll discover your own shorthand symbols and messages.

Core Message #34
Everyone is Connected to Everything and Everyone Else

We exist in an energy based universe. We may think of our physical world and the energy spiritual world as being two different things. We refer to the spiritual world, where our teams reside along with our dead friends and relatives, as "the great beyond," or "the other side," or "the afterlife." We draw these lines of distinction between us and them because of a lack of understanding about how the universe operates.

Again, I'll bring up our high school science and chemistry classes where we learned about atoms, those loosely based elements that form our world. It's sometimes difficult to accept that a rock or piece of granite, while appearing hard and solid, is actually tightly packed collections of always moving atoms, but that's how it works. And, everything, including us, is made of different combinations of the same stuff. The movement and vibration of those atoms allows everything to touch everything else, albeit in different ways and velocities.

It's not necessary at all to understand chemistry, physics, or math to build our psychic connections. That's a good thing for me, because those were never my best subjects in school. I'm more of a language arts type of guy. But, we do need to accept that everyone and everything is connected on the deepest possible level. The scientists continue to attempt to explain how everything works, and they continue to make valiant attempts, but I can tell you that they're not there, yet. They still haven't figured out how to explain everything that exists in our universe or how the universe actually works. While not a scientist, I can tell you quite frankly that we are in fact all energy beings, and we are connected to all other energy forms in our universe whether they are here in our physical world or on the other side.

Remember the telephone game we used to play as kids where we attached two tin cans with a piece of string and pretended we could talk to the person with the second can? Well, our psychic connection, in a crude description, is rather like that. We really can, with a little experience, learn to communicate with anyone who has ever lived a physical life. We can also communicate with other entities and beings who may or may not have lived in physical. I've had a few fun experiences with this.

The Seminar Drive

I'd been listening and connecting with the material offered by Abraham via Esther Hicks for some time and decided to attend a Law of Attraction workshop. While driving to the seminar, I got lost in a mountain park. I love to drive, and this loopy road through the mountains was the type of drive I often enjoy. But, I had somewhere to be, and I was in an unfamiliar place. I didn't know where I was and couldn't make sense of the map I had.

As I drove, I kept hearing this voice in my head saying: "Enjoy the Journey. Enjoy the Journey." The voice wasn't my own inner voice, and it wasn't the voice of any of my team members. Every time I had a negative thought about being late and missing the seminar, I again heard that other voice: "Enjoy the Journey. Enjoy the Journey." I suddenly realized it was Abraham speaking to me. When I acknowledged the voice as his, a great calmness came over me. I knew that I was fine. I started to enjoy the curving road through massive trees with occasional views through a valley all the way to the Pacific Ocean. It was lovely.

I reached the dead end of the road. I'd driven about thirty minutes. I knew I had to turn around, make my way back to where I'd started this drive, and then get on the correct road to the workshop. There was no way, based on the time on the clock, that I could accomplish that. Yet, I headed off in the "correct" direction with Abraham's words still repeating in my head: "Enjoy the journey." I can't explain how, but somehow, I arrived at the seminar more than forty-five minutes early.

Later, while going over the experience with my team, Abraham once again came into the scene saying that he knew I enjoyed beautiful drives, and that, if I hadn't gotten lost I never would have driven that lovely road through the trees, mountains, and beautiful vistas. For him, it was nothing to bend time a little to help me arrive at my destination with plenty of time to spare.

This was a wonderful awakening for me. The energy world, the spirit world, really is something we can't fully understand from our physical vantage point. We must simply accept that we don't understand it all and trust our team to guide us in positive ways.

The Psychic Johnny Carson

For about ten or twelve minutes during a psychic meditation, I found myself talking to Bea Arthur, Gilda Radner, Estelle Getty, Jim Belushi, Alan Ludden, and Madeline Kahn.

I think of Bea and Madeline often. That's how it started. My team asked me who I'd like to talk with, and the first person on my mind was Bea. She came right through with a nice smile and a husky voice. We talked about her life a bit. Next came Madeline. I just adore her. As we talked, they brought in the other stars. I felt like a psychic Johnny Carson as more dead celebrities stepped forward to chat.

I received several personal messages from them, but the most important and shareable is that stars and celebrities are just people, just folks like us. Yes, they've done fun and interesting things. They've had a little luck, a lot of Law of Attraction on their sides, but they're just people.

Everyone has the ability to do what they want, to travel in the circles they want, to have the experiences they want. It's those who want it most that get it most often. It doesn't make them better or more fulfilled. Hell, it doesn't even necessarily make them happier than anyone else. It just shows that they had a moment of wanting what came to them.

I found it interesting, too, that they all talked about their love of live performance over other venues and genre. While there are few recordings of their live events, they all talked about how much more they enjoyed the spontaneity of the moment when performing live.

So, what are these dead celebs up to now? Bea is acting like a guardian angel and nudger of the universe for her grandchildren. Gilda is watching over Gene Wilder a bit, laughing a lot with her friends on the other side, and contemplating returning to physical again. Estelle Getty is already back in physical. Jim Belushi has also returned to physical (somewhere in New Jersey). Madeline Kahn, well, she's contemplating returning to physical in a different realm. She said there are more places than our Earth to spend physical time. Most importantly, they're all laughing a lot.

The point of sharing these stories is that they're fun. They also show that we have the ability to connect beyond our team. We can connect with dead relatives, the guides and angels of others, and even with people we never knew in life. When we're open to the experience and our psychic connection is encouraged, there really aren't any limits to where we can travel during the experience. It doesn't matter if we connect with our team for personal knowledge and guidance or if we're just in search of a bit of fun and connecting with others who have traveled our universe. If we want to connect and interact with them, it's possible.

That said, it's also possible that the entity can't or won't come through. There are many reasons for this. They may not have a message to share. They may not have anything to say. Sometimes, especially when performing readings for others, someone will want to talk to a transitioned spouse or parent. The person they want to speak with will step forward, show themselves with recognizable details, and then not say anything at all. This can be frustrating. It's best if we trust them at that moment and trust that the best message they can share in the moment is only being present. They've filled the request of making a connection. We sometimes have to be happy with that, with what we get. There's no forcing those on the other side to do anything that isn't in our best interest, even if at the time we don't understand.

Core Message #35
We are Each a Part of the Conscious Evolution

While it's true that we're each on our own individual journey through both life and spirit, it's also true that the experience and knowledge we gain, both while we are in physical form and when we are in pure spirit, source energy, is a part of the collective conscious of all time. One term given to this collective knowledge is the Akashic Record. Edgar Cayce saw the Akashic Record as a giant encyclopedia, which he said he could tap into during his trance meditative state. I prefer to call this record of knowledge the collective conscious.

We all have access to this body of collective knowledge. When we come forth into physical, we arrive with a large amount of knowledge. We're ready, as soon as we learn a few basic motor skills (like walking and eating) and some language skills, to leap into life and continue our learning and growth as individuals.

It is because we arrive with a great amount of collective knowledge that we humans experience a type of generation gap. How amazed are older people when the young people pick up and quickly understand the latest technology? The generations before mine were master builders and creators. For my generation, we easily understood computer technology. The younger generations are immediate experts at social media and texting. There's no telling where the new and upcoming generations will take us.

Young people not only arrive with great knowledge, they also haven't yet been boxed in by old ways of thinking and doing. To them, anything is possible.

As we journey through our physical life, as we learn, experience, and grow, our knowledge and experience isn't only taken on by our spirit energy self. Our new knowledge and experience is added to the collective. This addition of material from billions of humans coming and going in our physical world is responsible for the constant growth and expansion of our universe.

As we build and grow our psychic connection, we have the opportunity to tap into the collective consciousness. Because of our connection, we lift the limits placed. Not only do we have access to our own knowledge and experience, but to the growing body of knowledge that is the current collective consciousness.

Core Message #36
We are not Required to Learn Anything on Our Life Journey

We enter our physical life with only one goal: to be happy. And, even that, while desired, isn't required. What you do with your life is your choice at this very moment. There's no "required" checklist of accomplishments (personal or otherwise).

One of the great misconceptions of human existence is that we've come into our physical lives to learn a required series of lessons and that we return over and over to physical existence to continue learning some required set of lessons, that we're doomed to return to physical life until we learn those lessons. This concept is false.

It's true that when we come into our physical life we do learn, grow, and expand. We are not required to do so. Instead, we have absolute free will, both while we are here in physical form and also when we are in pure energy form on the other side. We choose when we'll come into physical and when we leave. We choose all aspects of our life, no matter what form we're in.

Karma, as we've been taught about it, also does not exist. We are never required to return to a physical life to pay for a debt or unkindness or learn a specific lesson because of a harm we've caused someone else. Pure energy, the source of all existence, is a place of absolute and unconditional love. Our inner being, which remains mostly in pure energy form, is loved by all the other forms in pure energy and also feels great love toward us at all times. In truth, we can never do anything wrong during our time in physical. Instead, our time in physical is about pursuing our wants and desires on our life journey. Through those experiences, we learn, grow, and expand. This expansion and growth is not only our own, but also shared with the collective conscious.

When we come forth into our physical life, we do so to have the experience of life. We don't have a major, predestined plan for our time here. Instead, we're on a journey that changes as we move through life. The only goal of our life is to be as happy and joyous as possible. We arrive believing that life is supposed to be fun. When we leave the physical world and return to source, no matter what experiences we've had along our life journey, we will return to the belief that life is supposed to be fun.

It's important on our life journey to do all we can to let go of the "have tos," "woulds," and "shoulds." Most of these expectations are placed on us by others. Most of the time we find it easier to acquiesce to those expectations rather than rebel against them and pursue our own direction and desires in life. It's worth noting that doing so, living our lives because of the expectations of others, is like everything else, it's our personal choice.

Core Message #37
There's No Requirement that We Expose Ourselves as Psychic

As we discussed in the beginning, everyone is psychic. And, as we discussed recently, there are no requirements to life. Yet, the vast majority of those currently living physical lives on the planet do not know or accept that this is true. Because there's such a small percentage of people who accept their own psychic awareness as a reality, exposing yourself to others as being psychic or having a psychic connection may be difficult.

As with everything else in life, there is no correct or wrong decision. Whether you declare your psychic connection to those in your life is totally your own choice. Our teams don't care. They love and positively support us no matter what choices and decisions we make. They support and love us unconditionally, without any form of judgment. Their only goal as they participate in our life journey is to be there for us and to help us attain whatever we want.

Personally, I have an incredibly supportive group of

friends. Many of them are spiritually aware and several of them have an interest in psychics, astrologers, card readers, and other "new age" concepts. When my own psychic skills suddenly appeared, they were interested and supportive of my exploration of these abilities. Yet, at first, when I found myself suddenly psychic, I felt a twinge of fear about exposing myself and my skills. Once I got over those fears, once I exposed myself to my friends, they continuously supported me. Their support gave me the courage to share my skills and abilities with a greater circle of family and acquaintances.

The important thing to realize is that, if you want to come out to those in our life as psychic, your team will support that decision. If you don't want to come out as psychic and only use your psychic connection to enrich your own life, your team will support that decision as well.

The point here is that you have absolute control of what you do in your life. Our teams are here and available to us whenever and in whatever form we want them. And, our teams support us even if we don't acknowledge them.

Conclusion

Our psychic journey is a personal experience. Even if we choose to share our adventure with others, even if we choose to perform psychic readings for others, the journey we are experiencing is our own.

As I continued along my psychic path and began sharing my gift and abilities through readings for others, I found a greater passion for life than I've ever felt before. At first, I performed readings for my close friends. I also experienced many "drive by" readings while in public places.

Ultimately, I've turned my psychic abilities into a career. I started by offering phone readings, at first for free. I wasn't sure that my abilities we solid enough to warrant a fee. My friend, Victoria Laurie, offered to be an early phone guinea pig for me, but I declined. I was too intimidated to read for someone who has done thousands of readings, not to mention reading for the person who I feel was greatly responsible for my psychic door opening. Victoria played an important role in my suddenly psychic experiences.

After I'd done dozens of successful phone readings and discovered a successful question and answer reading style, I contacted Victoria. I was ready to try to do a reading for her. Our phone reading time was terrific. I answered her questions and shared the information that I received. She was happy and amazed by my ability. She offered her own endorsement which meant a great deal to me. After all, I have great respect for Victoria as a writer and psychic. Having her happy and supportive at the end of our reading time was a moment of positive validation for me. It was as if the circle of the previous eighteen months was completed, and I was ready to move forward with my new career as a psychic.

My life journey has taken me in many varied directions and experiences. I've traveled the world as a professional musician. I've worked in banking, finance, and nonprofit fundraising. I've run conferences and large scale events. I've published books and helped others fulfill their writing and publishing dreams. There have been so many directions and experiences that have filled my life. But, none of these have provided the passion that my psychic journey continues to offer.

Your own life may be a jagged journey, too. Or, your path might be a bit more straightforward. Yet, here you are, like me, exploring your psychic side.

Whether you've found yourself suddenly psychic or whether you've been on a psychic journey for some time, the psychic connection can always grow and strengthen. Based on all the psychics I've met, everyone's journey is not only different from all the others, but it's also continually growing and changing. Just as in our life journey, in our psychic journey, there's always more to learn and experience.

Follow your dreams, follow your passion, and encourage others to do the same!

Suddenly Psychic Resources

Edgar Cayce and the Association for Research and Enlightenment

http://www.edgarcayce.org

Edgar Cayce has been called the "sleeping prophet," the "father of holistic medicine," and the most documented psychic of the twentieth century. For more than forty years of his adult life, Cayce gave psychic "readings" to thousands of seekers while in an unconscious state, diagnosing illnesses and revealing lives lived in the past and prophecies yet to come.

Esther Hicks

http://www.abraham-hicks.com

Esther Hicks is an inspirational speaker and author. She co-authored eight books with her husband, Jerry Hicks. Together, they have presented Law of Attraction workshops for Abraham-Hicks Publications in up to sixty cities per year since 1987.

Max Highstein

http://www.maxhighstein.com

Max Highstein is an intuitive counselor, spiritual guide, and teacher with over forty years of study, training, and practice on the spiritual path. With deep compassion and understanding, he tunes into higher guidance and offers information and dynamic energy that goes directly to the heart of your issues and concerns.

Victoria Laurie

http://www.victorialaurie.com

Victoria Laurie is a bestselling author of both Adult Mystery and Children's Middle-grade Fantasy Adventure. She is also a world renowned professional psychic intuitive.

Jane Roberts

http://www.sethcenter.com

Jane Roberts was an American author, poet, psychic, and trance medium, or spirit medium, who channeled a personality named Seth. The publication of the Seth texts, known as the Seth Material, established her as one of the preeminent figures in the world of paranormal phenomena.

Author Biography

Las Vegas Psychic Intuitive Gregory A. Kompes became suddenly psychic in 2008. As he continues to develop his intuitive abilities he's discovered that he's actually been psychic his entire life. What's more, he's learned that everyone has the ability to improve and utilize their own psychic connection.

Gregory came out as a professional psychic in 2009 and has performed hundreds of professional psychic readings since then. He also conducts his popular *An Evening with Psychic Gregory* events in Las Vegas, NV.

Like everyone following a psychic journey, Gregory depends on aid from his collection of spirit guides that include his grandfather, Jimmy; educator, Brad; coordinator, Peter; the Archangel Michael, and The Three Sisters—a collection of ancient bearers of the light.

Gregory is a bestselling author with a BA in English Literature from Columbia University, New York, and an MS Ed. from California State University, East Bay.

Acknowledgements

No one travels their journey alone. I feel great love and gratitude for my team on the other side: Jimmy, Brad, Peter, Michael, and The Three Sisters.

Thanks to my friend Victoria Laurie for helping me nudge open my psychic door and offering advice along my suddenly psychic journey.

I'd like to offer a special thanks to my "guinea pig" friends, Tena Beth Thompson, Leslie E. Hoffman, Teresa Watts, Garry Buzick, Grace Andrews, and Douglas A. Davy who willingly and wittingly helped me explore along my journey.

Finally, love and thanks to Todd Isbell for his constant and unwavering love and support.

Follow your dreams, follow your passion, and inspire others to do the same.

Gregory

CPSIA information can be obtained
at www.ICGtesting.com
Printed in the USA
FFOW03n0516180218
45052003-45441FF

9 780979 361227